Experimental Advanced Airborne Research Lidar (EAARL) Data Processing Manual

By Jamie M. Bonisteel, Amar Nayegandhi, C. Wayne Wright, John C. Brock, and David B. Nagle

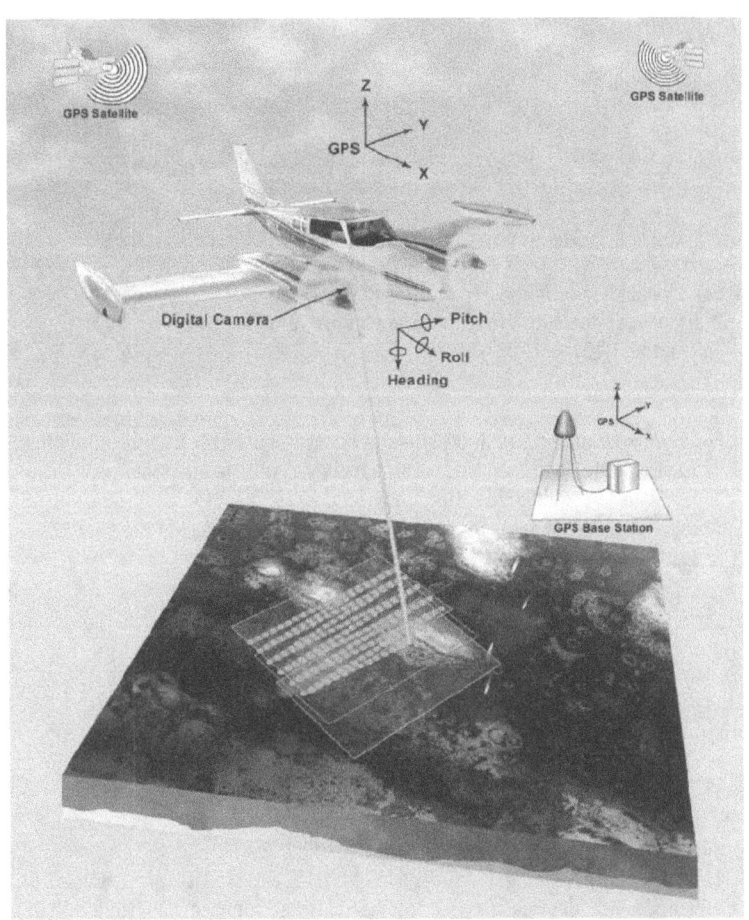

Open-File Report Series 2009–1078

U.S. Department of the Interior
U.S. Geological Survey

U.S. Department of the Interior
KEN SALAZAR, Secretary

U.S. Geological Survey
Suzette M. Kimball, Acting Director

U.S. Geological Survey, Reston, Virginia 2009

For product and ordering information:
World Wide Web: http://www.usgs.gov/pubprod
Telephone: 1-888-ASK-USGS

For more information on the USGS—the Federal source for science about the Earth,
its natural and living resources, natural hazards, and the environment:
World Wide Web: http://www.usgs.gov
Telephone: 1-888-ASK-USGS

Suggested citation:
Bonisteel, J.M., Nayegandhi, Amar, Wright, C.W., Brock, J. C., and Nagle, D.B., 2009, Experimental
Advanced Airborne Research Lidar (EAARL) Data Processing Manual: U.S. Geological Survey
Open-File Report, 2009-1078, 38p.

Experimental Advanced Airborne Research Lidar (EAARL) Data Processing Manual

By Jamie M. Bonisteel, Amar Nayegandhi, C. Wayne Wright, John C. Brock, and David B. Nagle

Open-File Report Series 2009–1078

U.S. Department of the Interior
U.S. Geological Survey

Contents

Figures

Tables

Experimental Advanced Airborne Research Lidar (EAARL) Data Processing Manual

By Jamie M. Bonisteel, Amar Nayegandhi, C. Wayne Wright, John C. Brock, and David Nagle

Introduction

The Experimental Advanced Airborne Research Lidar (EAARL) is an example of a Light Detection and Ranging (Lidar) system that utilizes a blue-green wavelength (532 nanometers) to determine the distance to an object. The distance is determined by recording the travel time of a transmitted pulse at the speed of light (fig. 1). This system uses raster laser scanning with full-waveform (multi-peak) resolving capabilities to measure submerged topography and adjacent coastal land elevations simultaneously (Nayegandhi and others, 2009).

This document reviews procedures for the post-processing of EAARL data using the custom-built Airborne Lidar Processing System (ALPS). ALPS software was developed in an open-source programming environment operated on a Linux platform. It has the ability to combine the laser return backscatter digitized at 1-nanosecond intervals with aircraft positioning information. This solution enables the exploration and processing of the EAARL data in an interactive or batch mode. ALPS also includes modules for the creation of bare earth, canopy-top, and submerged topography Digital Elevation Models (DEMs). The EAARL system uses an Earth-centered coordinate and reference system that removes the necessity to reference submerged topography data relative to water level or tide gages (Nayegandhi and others, 2006).

The EAARL system can be mounted in an array of small twin-engine aircraft that operate at 300 meters above ground level (AGL) at a speed of 60 meters per second (117 knots). While other systems strive to maximize operational depth limits, EAARL has a narrow transmit beam and receiver field of view (1.5 to 2 milliradians), which improves the depth-measurement accuracy in shallow, clear water but limits the maximum depth to about 1.5 Secchi disk depth (~20 meters) in clear water. The laser transmitter [Continuum EPO-5000 yttrium aluminum garnet (YAG)] produces up to 5,000 short-duration (1.2 nanosecond), low-power (70 microjoules) pulses each second. Each pulse is focused into an illumination area that has a radius of about 20 centimeters on the ground. The pulse-repetition frequency of the EAARL transmitter varies along each across-track scan to produce equal cross-track sample spacing and near uniform density (Nayegandhi and others, 2006).

Targets can have varying physical and optical characteristics that cause extreme fluctuations in laser backscatter complexity and signal strength. To accommodate this dynamic range, EAARL has the real-time ability to detect, capture, and automatically adapt to each laser return backscatter. The backscattered energy is collected by an array of four high-speed waveform digitizers connected to an array of four sub-nanosecond photodetectors. Each of the four photodetectors receives a finite range of the returning laser backscatter photons. The most sensitive channel receives 90% of the photons, the least sensitive receives 0.9%, and the middle channel receives 9% (Wright and Brock, 2002). The fourth channel is available for detection but is not currently being utilized. All four channels are digitized simultaneously into 65,536 samples for every laser pulse. Receiver optics consists of a 15-centimeter-diameter dielectric-coated Newtonian telescope, a computer-driven raster scanning mirror oscillating at 12.5 hertz (25 rasters per second), and an array of sub-nanosecond photodetectors. The signal emitted

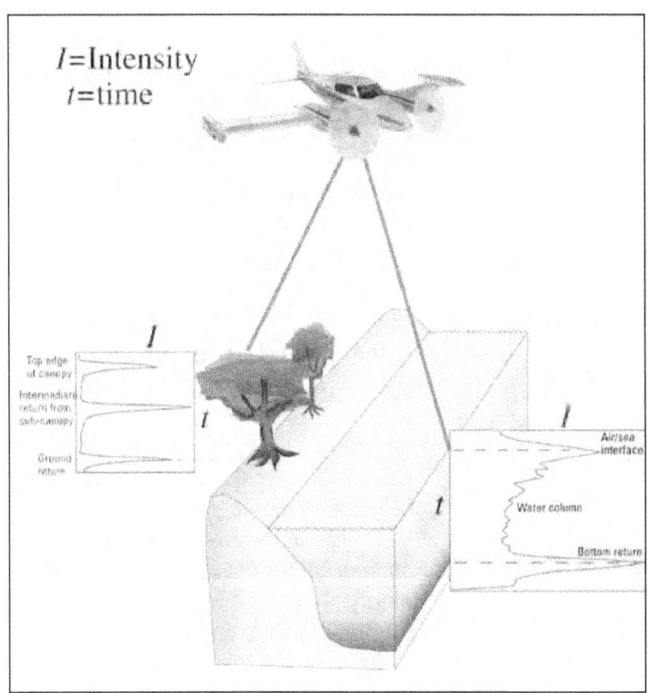

Figure 1. Sample waveform returns from vegetation and submerged topography (Wright and Brock, 2002).

by the pulsed laser transmitter is amplified as backscatter by the optical telescope receiver. The photomultiplier tube (PMT) then converts the optical energy into electrical impulses (Nayegandhi and others, 2006).

In addition to the full-waveform resolving laser, the EAARL sensor suite includes a down-looking 70-centimeter-resolution Red-Green-Blue (RGB) digital network camera, a high-resolution color infrared (CIR) multispectral camera (14-centimeter-resolution), two precision dual-frequency kinematic carrier-phase global positioning system (GPS) receivers, and an integrated gyroscope-based, miniature digital inertial measurement unit (IMU) that provides accurate attitude information (Nayegandhi and others, 2006).

Laser error depends on the type of surface being mapped, which can range from a few centimeters in open canopies to several meters in closed and sloping terrains. Recent studies have shown that EAARL elevation root mean square errors (RMSE) range from 10 to 14 centimeters for submerged topography to 16 to 20 centimeters for sub-canopy topography. The RMSE is also highly dependent on GPS satellite configuration and lidar sampling angles. A high RMSE occurs during poor satellite configuration and large sampling angles that usually happen at the edge of the swath (Nayegandhi and others, 2009).

Processing of Raw EAARL Data

For waveform-resolving instruments such as EAARL, the range is determined in post-processing. Processing algorithms have been developed to extract the range to the first and last significant return. The shape of the waveform is determined by a number of sensor parameters and backscattering properties of targets. Some important sensor parameters include the shape of the laser pulse, the receiver impulse function, and parameters describing pulse spreading (Wagner and others, 2007). Standard pulse-detection methods include threshold (rising edge of signal exceeds given threshold), center of gravity (computed over all points above fixed threshold), maximum zero crossing of second derivative (detection of local maxima), and constant fraction (the zero crossings of the difference between an attenuated and a time-delayed version of the signal) (Wagner and others, 2004).

Problems occur when waveforms have complex forms and backscattered pulses are low when compared to noise levels. Algorithms are adjusted to tasks to account for waveform complexity (Wagner and others, 2004). ALPS uses the following algorithms to differentiate between returns: the zero crossing of the second derivative is used to detect the first return and the trailing-edge algorithm is used to detect the range to the last return; that is, the algorithm searches for the location prior to the last return where the direction changes along the trailing edge (Nayegandhi and others, 2006).

ALPS has the ability to analyze and process the data collected by the EAARL system in an interactive or batch mode. Some interactive modules in ALPS include: pre-survey flight line definition, flight path plotting, topography data generation, lidar raster and waveform examination, and digital camera image playback. ALPS in the batch processing module will automatically generate topography data. This automation eliminates the time-consuming effort of interactively generating topography data.

Interactive Processing Mode

In order to begin interactive processing, the following steps assume the user is logged into the computer where the raw data are stored. See Appendices A, B, and C for possible steps preceding the initial interactive processing.

Opening ALPS Processing Windows

Start a terminal session. The user must migrate to the *src* directory to begin all processing in ALPS.

Type in the command line: **cd / opt/eaarl/lidar-processing/src** [press *enter*].

Start yorick session by typing in the command line: **./ytk eaarl.ytk l1pro. ytk** [press *enter*].

Figure 2. ALPS provides an interface for data processing, visualization, and investigation.

The *ytk, eaarl*, and *Process EAARL Data* windows will open. Opening these windows will load a series of files necessary for ALPS functions (fig. 2).

Loading the EAARL Database File

To load the EAARL Database file (EDB), go to the *eaarl window* and select *file >> Load EAARL Database Index (Edb)*. The data are stored by mission day within each mission directory. Migrate to the *EAARL* subdirectory within the selected mission day [for example, */training/raw/HR_ KATRINA/20050908/eaarl/*] and select the *idx* file [click *Open*]. After the *idx* file is loaded the user will see the following: *This will set 'gps_time_correction' to -14.0* (only if the data were collected after 1 January, 2006, otherwise it will be -13.0).

An *edb* window will open with information about the dataset. Similar information is listed in the open terminal window (fig. 3). The *EAARL* window becomes the *Current Data* window.

A window regarding the digital camera playback will open, *Digital Camera Playback Software isn't running. Would*

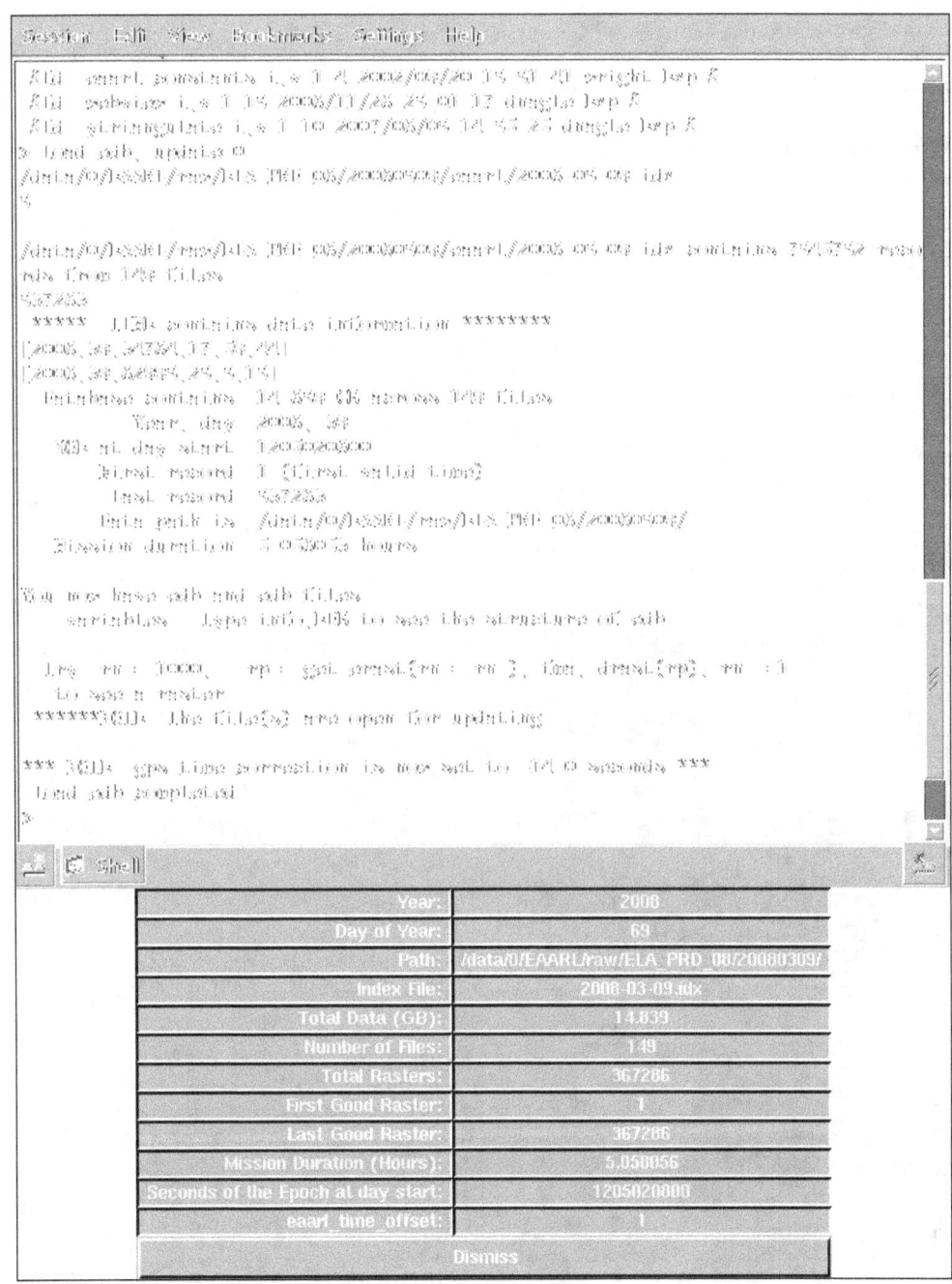

Figure 3. EAARL database index windows.

you like to run it now? Select *Yes.* The *RGB* window appears. To set up the RGB camera to view images acquired during or after the year 2007, go to the *RGB* window and select *File >> Select Path.* Select the *cam1* directory [click *OK*]. For any images acquired before 2007, go to the RGB window and select *File >> Select File.* Select the *cam1.tar* file within that mission day (*/training/raw/HR_KATRINA/20050908/2005-cam1. tar*).

A window will open, indicating the camera is mounted. This window will close when all of the .tar files are loaded (this may take a minute). This selection will allow the user to pair lidar rasters, waveforms, and images together. Press the forward/backward arrows or drag the crossbar in the RBG window to view the rest of the images collected on that day (fig. 4). The images are collected at an interval of 1 per second(s).

Select *Dismiss* to close the *edb* window. To access the window later, go to the *File* menu in the *Current Data* window and select *Edb status* (fig. 3).

Loading GPS Flight Track Information

To load flight track information, go to the *Current Data* window and select *Maps/Nav >> Plotting Tool.* In the window that opens (fig. 5), select the *Settings* tab and choose a coordinate system by selecting *UTM* or *Lat/Lon* in the *Coordinates* drop-down menu (click to select).

To load the current precision GPS flight track file, go to the *Plotting Tool* window (fig. 5) and select the *PNAV* tab >> *Load Track.* The flight day directory window will open. Select the *trajectories* directory. This *trajectories* directory window can also be opened by going to the *File* menu of the *Current Data* window and selecting *Load GPS PNAV data.* Select the most recent *cmb-pnav* directory (with *p* in title) [click *Open*].

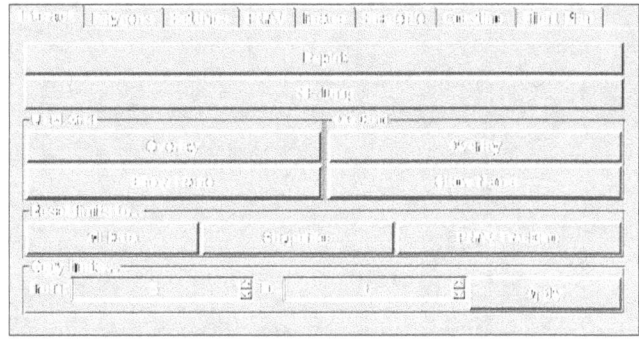

Figure 5. The Plotting Tool window manages flight lines, shapefiles, coastal base maps, and flight plans.

The naming scheme of the selected GPS file should be similar to the following example: YYYY-MM-DD-p-YYYY-MM-DD-zny1-wgs84-cmb-pnav (table 1). When the pnav directory window opens, select the *.ybin* file [click *Open*]. If a precision pnav is not selected, then a warning window will appear stating: *The pnav file you have selected does not appear to be a precision trajectory. It should not be used in the production of final data products or to assess accuracy of the system.i.* The precision pnav file accounts for all of the errors in the GPS system. See *www.ngs.noaa.gov/orbits* or *http://igscb.jpl.nasa.gov/igscb/center/analysis/noaa.acn* for further details on GPS processing.

Table 1. GPS satellite ephemeride file indicators.

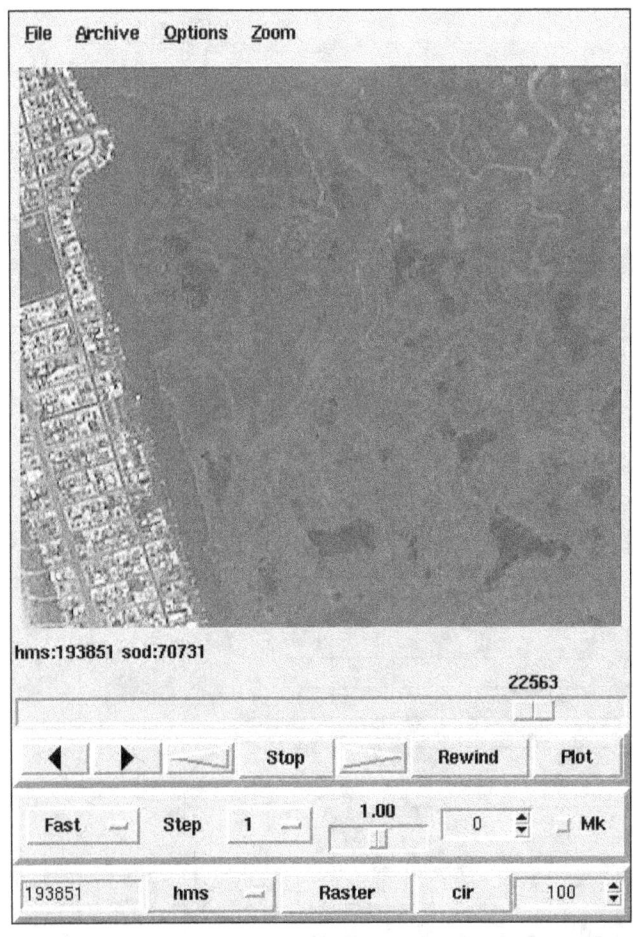

Figure 4. An image from the RGB camera.

GPS Solution	Availability From Last Observation	Accuracy
U - Ultra	6 hours	~ 20-40 cm
R - Rapid	17 hours	~ 4-7 cm
B - Broadcast	24 hours	~ 1.6 m
P - Precision	4 -10 days	~ 2-5 mm

Loading Digital Miniature Attitude Reference System (DMARS) Information

Next, the Digital Miniature Attitude Reference System (DMARS) must be loaded. This Inertial Measurement Unit (IMU) is used for precise-attitude determination. Load the information from the *Current Data* window by selecting *File >> Load DMARS Attitude data* or *>> Maps/Nav >> Load DMARS data*. The trajectories window will appear again. Select the most recent *-ins* directory [click *Open*]. When the *ins* directory window opens, select the *ins.pbd* file [click *Open*].

The command window should reflect all data that is loaded (fig. 6). The applied GPS correction time, minimum and maximum values for the Seconds of the Week (SOW), Position Dilution of Precision (PDOP), Root Mean Square Error (RMSE), latitude, longitude, and altitude are shown. All loaded files are also listed.

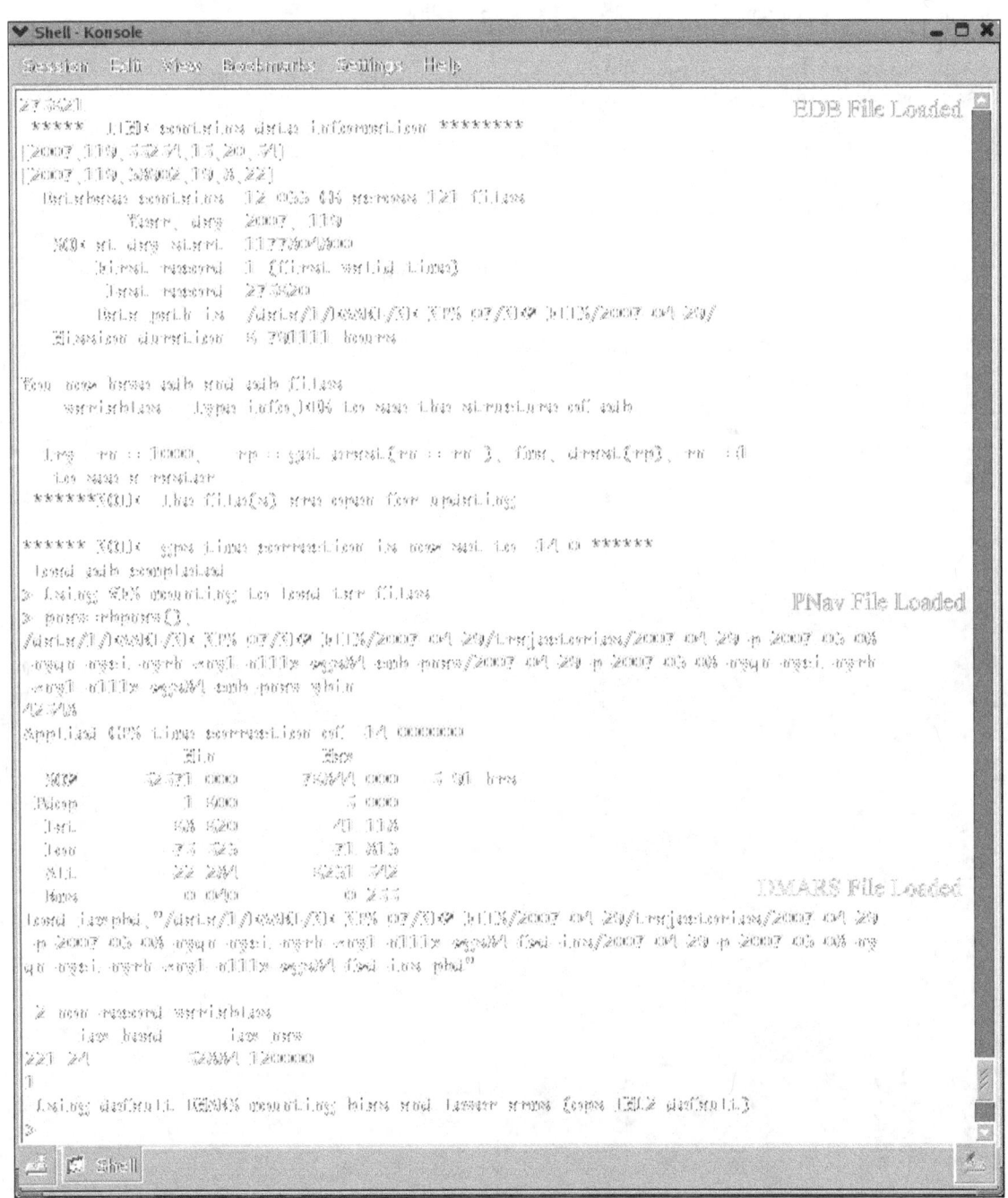

Figure 6. Yorick shell after the EDB, PNav, and DMARS files have been loaded.

Position Dilution of Precision is the measure of the geometrical strength of the GPS satellite configuration. This is the amount of error in the GPS position. A PDOP less than 4 results in the best accuracy (under 1 meter). A PDOP higher than 4 may be displayed, but it is likely the EAARL system was not collecting data at that time.

Loading Mission Constants

To load mission constants, go to the *Current Data* window and select *Settings >> Load Ops_conf Settings*. A window will open showing the current directory. Select the *ops_conf-YYYYMMDD.i* file [click *Open*]. If an ops_conf file does not exist for each day of flight, navigate to a different directory to select the file (usually up one directory, to the mission directory). This indicates only one ops_conf file was created for the entire mission. To determine the loaded mission constants, type ops_conf in the command line or in the *Current Data* window, select *Settings >> Current Ops_conf Settings*.

Viewing Flight Lines

To view flight lines, click *Plot Track* on the *PNAV* tab on the *Plotting Tool* window (fig. 7). On the *Yorick 6* window, left

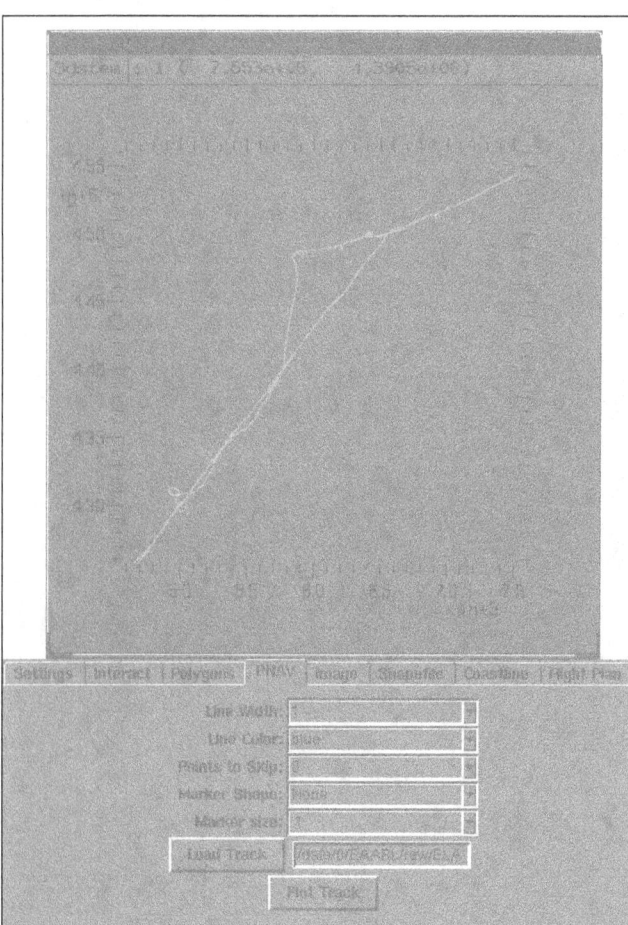

Figure 7. Flight lines window.

click to zoom in and right click to zoom out. Middle click (or control left click) and hold to pan. Customize the flight line view by using the *Plotting Tool* window (fig. 5) to adjust the line width, line color, points to skip, marker shape, and marker size (table 2). Some collection days will cross Universal Transverse Mercator (UTM) zones, and that flight line data will not plot in the window. In this case, the shell will inform the user that *Selected flight line crosses UTM Zones*. To view flight lines from a specific UTM zone, type **curzone=#** [for example, **curzone=16**] in the command line. Only that portion of the flight lines collected in that zone will plot in the *Yorick 6* window.

Loading Coastal Base Maps

To load coastal base maps, click *Add coastline map* under the *Coastline* tab of the *Plotting Tool* window. This will

Table 2. Interact tab for the Plotting Track window functions.

Feature	Functionality	Command Line Functions
Reset Limits to…	Resets the viewing window to all data, shapefiles, and PNAV tracklines.	Another way to restore all of the loaded information on the active window is to type **limits** or **window, #; limits** [**window, 1; limits**].
Clear and Plot	Refreshes the selected window.	
SF Jump	Allows the user to select to point on the displayed flight line. The command terminal will list information about the selected area. The Red-Green-Blue (RGB) camera image will jump to this selected area.	Set the Universal Transverse Mercator (UTM) zone by typing **curzone=#** in the command terminal [for example, **curzone=16**].
Overlay	Displays a UTM or quarter quadrangle grid over the data.	
Show Grid Name	Lists given UTM or quarter quadrangle grid name. After the grid has been overlaid onto data, click on the active data window.	
Copy limits…	Apply the limits from one window to another.	

provide a visual map of the flight line locations. Select the *pbd* directory (*/opt/eaarl/lidar-processing/maps/pbd/*) to see a list of *.pbd* files from around the world. Pick the appropriate file depending on the region from which the data were collected. For example, choose *med-res-eusa.pbd* for the Long Island area. Select *fla.pbd* for the State of Florida coastline map. Once the coastline is chosen, click *Plot coastline maps*. The following information may appear on the command window: *Selected Base Map Crosses # UTM Zones. Select Zone Number from # to #: Enter Zone Number*. Input a zone number here [for example, **16**] and press *enter*. The *Yorick 6* window will load the base map. To change zones, go to the *Interact* tab and click *Clear and Plot*.

Viewing Raster Images and Waveforms

To load the raster images, go to the *Lidar* menu on the *Current Data* window and select *Examine Lidar Rasters*. The *drast* window will appear. Click *Raster* on the *RGB* camera window. This will display an unreferenced raster image for that area (fig. 8). The field of view of the RGB camera slightly exceeds the length of the raster scan. A raster represents one side of the oscillating scan (one zig or one zag) (fig. 9). Using the *drast* window, the user can press play or drag the crossbar to view the rest of the raster images collected. Click the *Animate GeoRef* button to obtain the georeferenced raster image for that particular RGB image displayed (fig. 8).

To analyze waveforms for the unreferenced raster image, click *Examine Waveforms* in the *drast* window. The command window will state *Window: 1. Left Click: Examine Waveform. Middle click: Exit.* By left clicking on the raster image in several locations, the user will see that waveforms change.

Loading Other Images

Rather than overlaying the flight lines onto a base map, the user may want to overlay the flight lines onto an image. To load other images, go to the *Image* tab in the *Plotting*

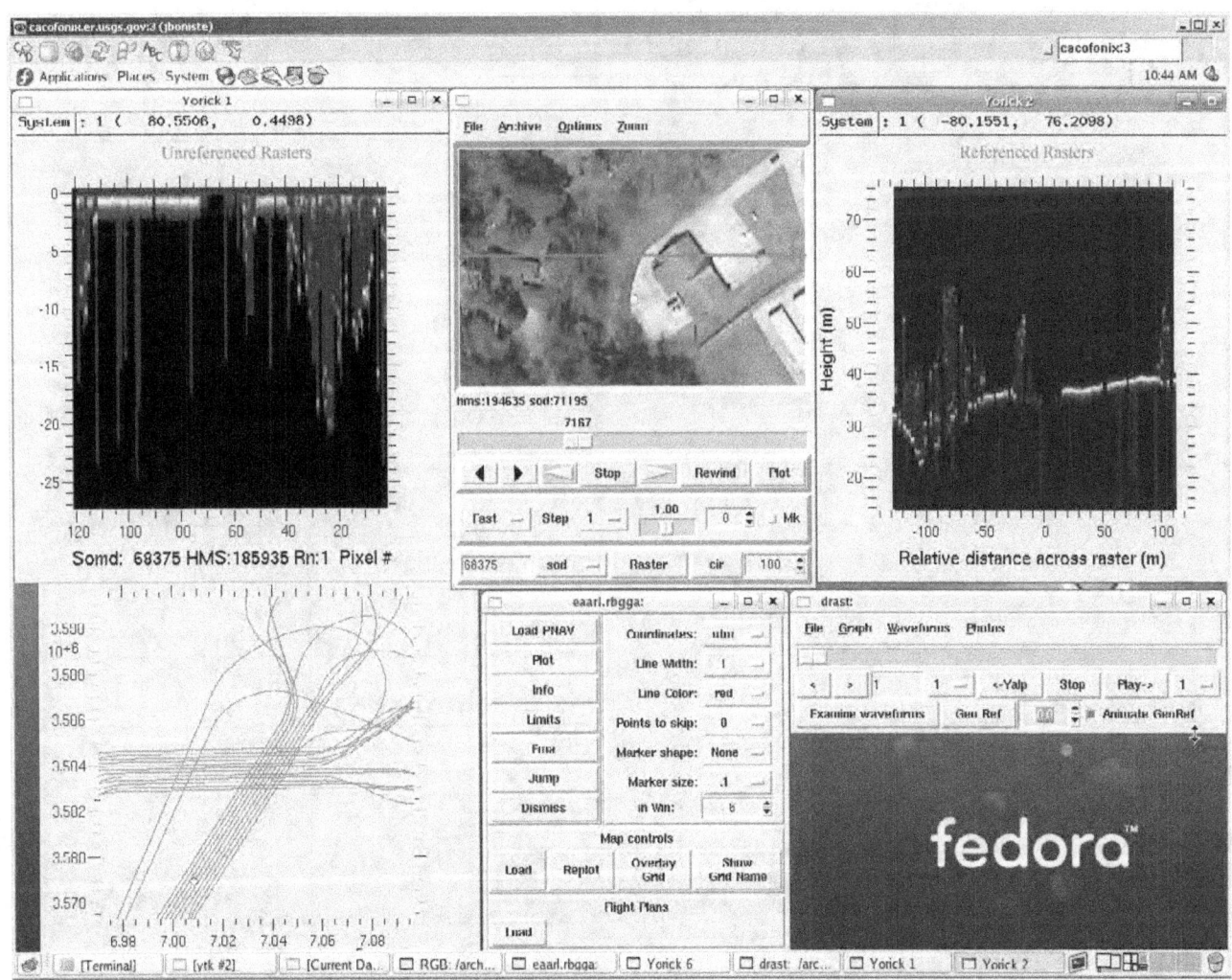

Figure 8. Screenshot from an interactive session in ALPS showing EAARL rasters (top right and left), RGB (top center) images, and flight line map (bottom left).

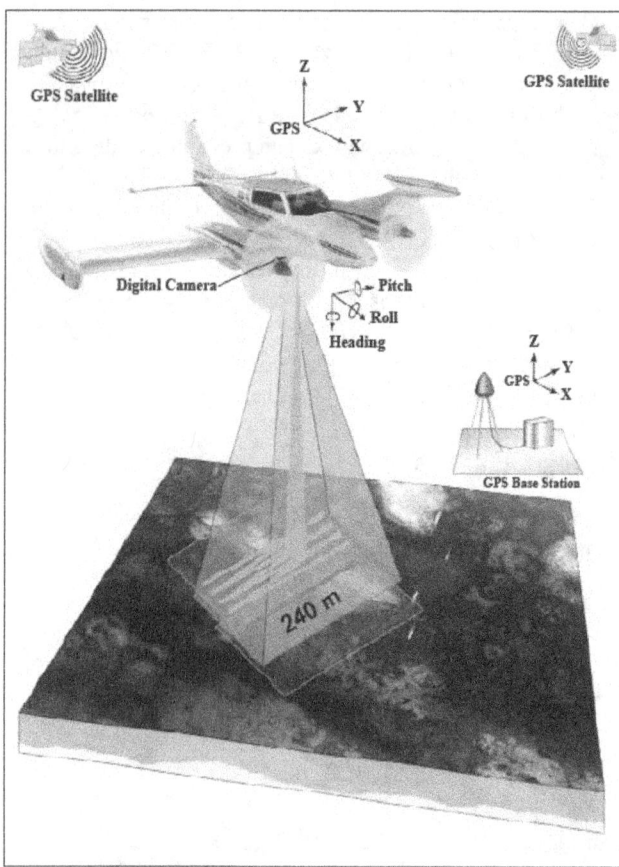

Figure 9. An illustration of the EAARL oscillating scan pattern and aircraft positioning (Brock and others, 2004).

Tool window. Select *Add image with world file, Add image, specifying location, or Add lidar image.* In the new window that opens, navigate to the directory that contains the image. It will automatically search for *.jpg*, but *.png*, *.gif*, and *.tif* files can also be viewed by changing the file type at the bottom of the window.

Click *Plot Images* in order to view the image in the defined *Yorick 6* window location.

RGB Camera Functions

To view and manipulate the RGB images, follow the instructions in table 3.

CIR Camera Functions

To load and view CIR images, go to the *Current Data* window and select *1-Hz CIR High-Res Images* from the *Imagery* menu. A window will open that allows the user to navigate to the directory where the CIR images are located. Select the *cir* directory within the mission day directory [click *OK*]. A blank window will appear. To view the CIR images, move the slider bar to a point in the flight on the RGB window. Then click on the *cir* button in the RGB window.

Table 3. Red-Green-Blue (RGB) camera functions.

Feature	Functionality
Arrow keys or slider bar	Moves through the flight line images (fig. 4).
◁▷	Plays continuously through the RGB images.
Stop	Ends continuous play.
Rewind	Returns the viewer to the first image of data collection.
Plot	Shows the user where the image is located in the flight line data. In the window where the flight lines are displayed, a blue triangle will appear (fig. 7).
Fast	Changes speed at which the images are continuously viewed.
Step	Determines how many images are skipped at once. For example, if '2' is selected, then the user will skip ahead or back two images at a time.
1.00	Moving the slider bar will alter the brightness of the image. This function is located next to the Step function.
0	Syncs RGB and Color-Infrared (CIR) images if they are displayed separately from one another.
Mk	Marks a particular image. Can move through only the marked images.
181800 hms	Can select specific RGB images by entering in a value in this space. Depress the 'hms' button to display the value in hours, minutes, and seconds (hms), seconds of the day (sod), or image index (cin).
Raster	Pairs an RGB image with a raster scan.
CIR	Pairs CIR images with RGB images.
100	Changes the zoom factor of the RGB image. The lowest possible value is '1' and the highest possible value is '200'.

The image in the RGB window will then appear in the blank window (fig. 10). The CIR images can be viewed and manipulated as follows (table 4).

Figure 10. An image from the CIR camera.

Topographic Lidar Data Processing

To begin the processing of EAARL lidar data, the user must zoom in on the flight lines shown in the *Yorick 6* window. Select a small area with at least two flight lines. Select flight lines for processing by going to the *Define Region* drop-down menu in the top panel of the *Process EAARL Data* window. Select one of the following choices:

Points in Polygon – This function is used to select any kind of polygonal shape. This method is the easiest way to select as little or as much of a desired area as is needed.

Rubberband Box – This function will automatically create a rectangular-shape box from the northwest corner when dragged across the screen.

Rectangular Coords – This function will process a specific area with known latitude/longitude or UTM coordinates (fig. 11).

If the *Points in Polygon* method is selected, a message appears as follows, *Draw a Polygon in Window 6 to define a region using a series of left mouse clicks. To complete the polygon, middle mouse click or <Ctrl> and left mouse click.* [click *OK*]. To select an area, complete a series of left clicks that creates a polygon and center click to finish the polygon.

If the *Rubberband Box* method is selected, a message appears as follows, *Drag a Rectangular Box in Window 6 to define region.* [click *OK*]. To select an area, left click, drag across the flight lines, and then release to complete the box.

If the *Rectangular Coords* method is selected, the *l1widc* window will open. Select either *LatLon* or *UTM* from the *Coordinate System* drop-down menu. Type in the *UTM Zone*,

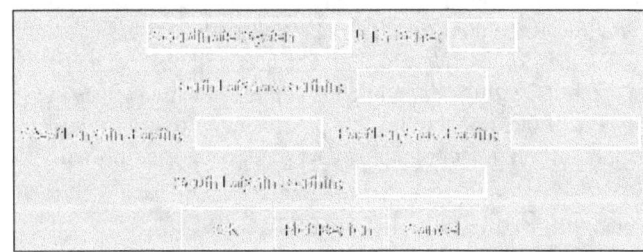

Figure 11. Rectangular coordinate (l1widc window) method.

Table 4. Color-Infared (CIR) camera functions.

Feature	Functionality
Center or right click on the CIR image.	Opens CIR menu.
Left click on CIR image.	Moves onto the next collected image (fig. 10).
	Alters the brightness of the image.
	Controls the size of the image. A value of '15' yields the smallest image while a value of '1' yield the largest image. Located beneath the slider bar.
	Changes the number of images to skip.
	Shows when the image was collected in flight in hms as well as sod.
Next	Moves forward through the images. It will move through the number of selected skipped images.
Prev	Moves backward through the images. It will move through the number of selected skipped images.
Play	Moves forward continuously through the images. It will move through the number of skipped images.
Yalp	Moves backward continuously through the images. It will move through the number of skipped images.
RGB	Aligns the RGB image with the selected CIR image.

North Lat/Max.Northing, *South Lat/Min.Northing*, *West Lon/Min.Easting*, and *East Lon/Max.Easting*. Click *Plot Region* (Click *OK*).

If the *Points in Polygon* or *Rubberband Box* method is selected, draw a polygon or a box over the flight lines. Once drawn, the command window will list how many records and seconds of data are included. Processing time increases substantially if the selected area is too large. An area that includes less than 300 s of data is most efficient.

Next, select *Topo Under Veg* in the data type drop-down menu, located next to the *Define Region* drop-down menu. This mode is chosen unless processing for submerged topography. (See the Submerged Topography (Bathymetry) Lidar Data Processing with Waveform Investigation section for processing details.) *Topo Under Veg* processes both first and last returns. Other choices for processing the data include *Multi Peak Veg* and *Direct. Wave Spectra*. (See appendix E for discussion on these processing choices.)

It is not necessary to use the *Method* drop-down menu or the *in Win:* menu in the top panel of the *Process EAARL Data* window. Keep the *Correct Range Walk with Centroid* selected. Click the *Process Now* button. The user will observe a *Flight Segment Progress Bar* while the command window lists the details of the topographic data processing. A return [>] will appear when the topographic data processing has finished.

Viewing Processed Topography Data

To view processed topography data, go to the *Process EAARL Data* window to choose one of the variables from the *Variable* drop-down menu in the middle panel. Select *veg_all* for viewing first or last returns. Choose *First Return Topography* or *Bare Earth Topography*, respectively, in the *Mode* drop-down menu. Other *Mode* options include:

- *Surface Amplitude* – This mode shows the backscatter from the first waveform channel.

- *Bottom Amplitude* – This mode shows the backscatter from the last waveform channel.

- *Canopy Height* – This mode represents the distance from the first return to the bare ground.

Do not adjust the *in Win:* drop-down menu in the middle panel of the *Process EAARL Data* window. Click the *Auto Fma* button to plot with a fresh screen each time the *Plot* button is pressed. Click the *Histogram Elevations* button. The *Yorick 7* window will open with a histogram displaying the elevation range of data in WGS84 (G1150) elevations (fig. 12). The *Color Bar Tool* window will also open. On the *Color Bar Tool*, select the *Both* button. Click the location on the histogram that corresponds to the minimum elevation, *Cmin*, and then choose the maximum elevation, *Cmax*. The minimum elevation can be selected separately by clicking *Cmin* and selecting the location on the histogram. The same can be done to select a location for maximum elevation, *Cmax*. Click *Plot* and a window will open with a view of processed data. These data are unfiltered, so

noise may be visible. Elevations higher than *Cmax* will appear white, while elevations lower than *Cmin* will not appear.

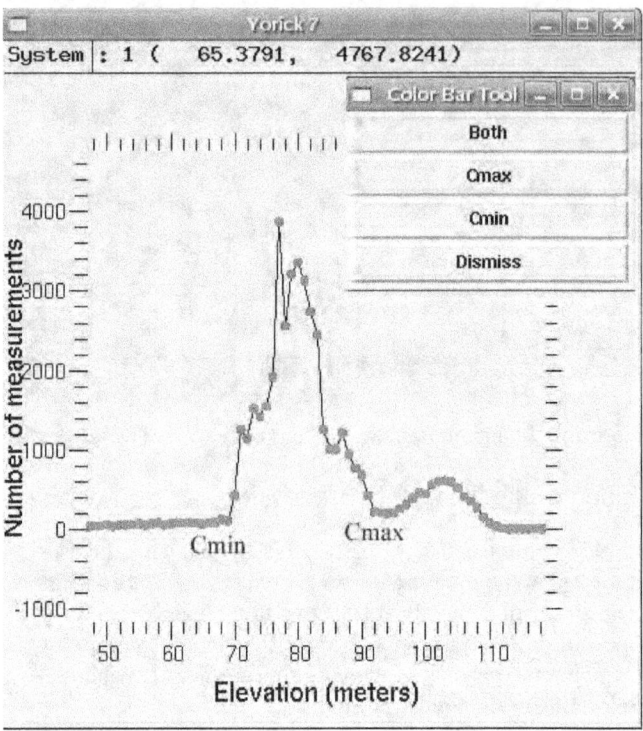

Figure 12. A histogram display and color bar tool window.

To link the processed topography data with the waveforms, raster images, and RGB images, press the *Pixel Waveform* button in the middle panel of the *Process EAARL Data* window. Left click on the window with the processed topography data to examine a point, center click to set as a reference point, and right click to quit. When left clicking over the topography data points, two windows will open. One will display the waveform for that data point and another will display the raster image (fig. 13). The waveform, raster, and the RGB camera windows are all georeferenced together. Right click on the processed topography data to quit the pixel waveform module.

The sample waveform window in figure 13 represents a sandy region with coastal vegetation. The display shows all three channels: black (90%), red (9%), and blue (0.9%). The x-axis displays digital counts, which represent the amplitude or relative backscatter. The digital count values are inverted in the EAARL receiver hardware. The values decrease with an increase in backscatter return signal strength (Nayegandhi and others, 2006).

The raster scan consists of 120 laser pulses along a zig or zag approximately normal to the flight path. The raster is a false-color image of the backscatter return signal for the most sensitive channel. Bright colors indicate high signal strength. The vertical stripes in the scan indicate that the laser pulse does not have recorded data (Nayegandhi and others, 2006).

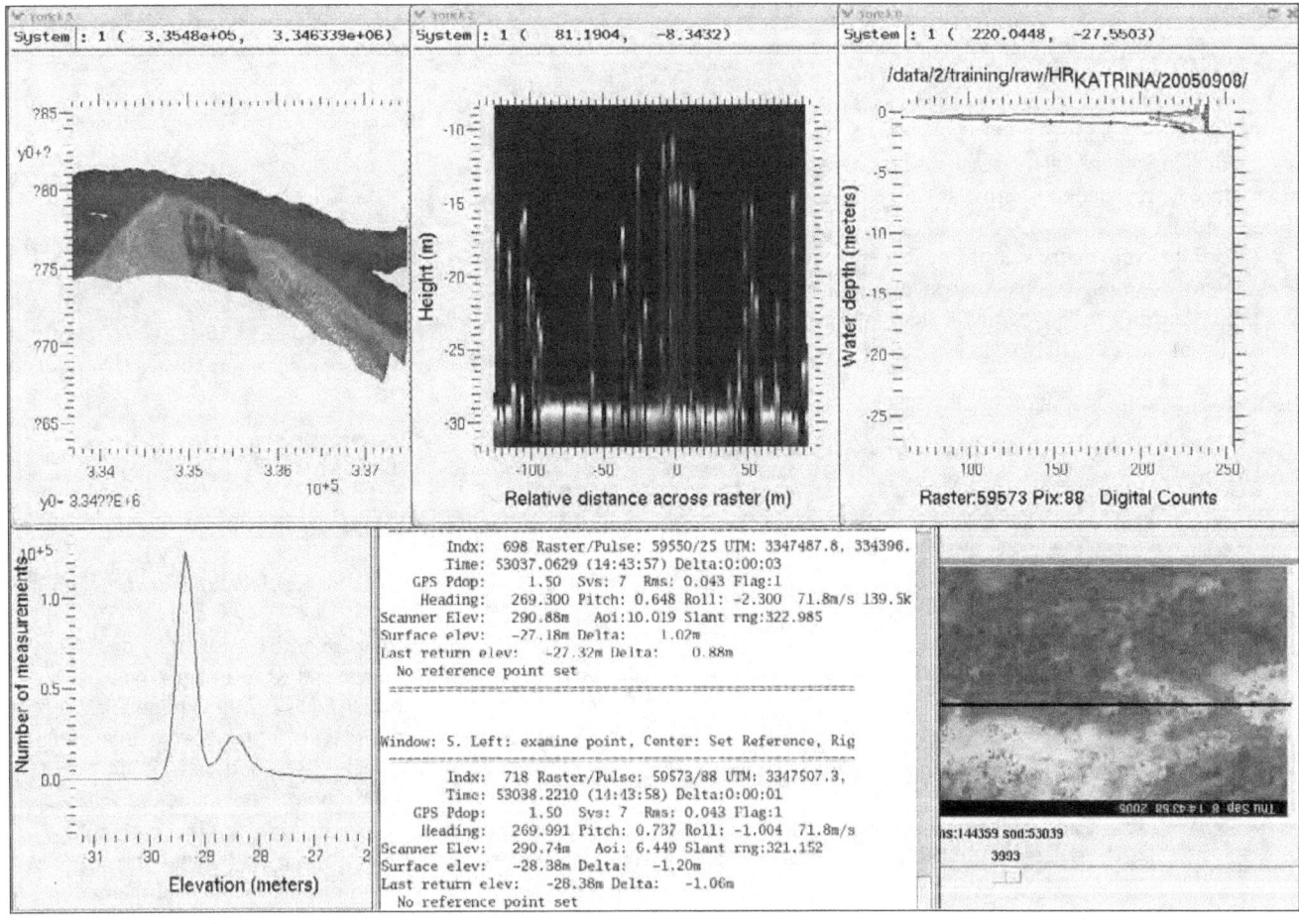

Figure 13. A screenshot showing processed data (top left), a georeferenced raster image (top center), a sample waveform (top right), a histogram (bottom left), the ALPS command window (bottom center), and an RGB image (bottom right).

Submerged Topography (Bathymetry) Lidar Data Processing with Waveform Investigation

Water surface specular reflection (Fresnel reflection) usually occurs near nadir, along the scan pattern. Fresnel's equations describe the behavior of light when it moves between media of differing refractive indices. These reflections are represented by a strong-amplitude backscatter signal, usually saturated in the most sensitive channel, while the range is then resolved in the least sensitive channel. The water surface elevation is estimated by determining the range of all Fresnel reflections within a scan and extrapolating these values for the entire length of scan. The sea bottom is determined by correcting for the following: refraction of the incident laser pulse at the air-water interface, change in the speed of light as it enters the water column, the attenuation of the laser signal in water, and the effect of water column turbidity on the laser backscatter. To determine the bottom, corrections are performed by examining the sample waveforms from different locations in the survey area to define constants for exponential decay. The data are processed in reference to the WGS84 (G1150) ellipsoid datum, which is independent of the elevation of the water surface (Nayegandhi and others, 2006).

Interactive processing for submerged topography is similar to topographic processing with a few adjustments and additions. Complete the previous steps in the Interactive Processing Mode sections. Also review the Topographic Lidar Data Processing and the Viewing Processed Topography Data sections of this manual for the following repeated steps.

Zoom in to a small area of the loaded flight lines in the *Yorick 6* window. Select the flight lines by going in the *Define Region* drop-down menu on the *Process EAARL Data* window. Select one of the following tools:

- Points in Polygon

- Rubberband Box

- Rectangular Coords

Once a tool is chosen, a window will open discussing the selection. If the *Points in Polygon* tool was selected, draw a polygon over the flight lines. Select *Submerged Topo* in the drop-down menu located next to the *Define Region* drop-down menu. An alternate method for viewing the submerged topography data is also available. See appendix E for details on the *Direct. Wave Spectra* mode.

It is not necessary to use the *Method* drop-down menu or the *in Win:* menu. Keep *Correct Range Walk with Centroid* and *Use Fresnel reflections to determine water surface* buttons selected. *Use Fresnel reflections to determine water surface* should not be selected in riverine or coastal environments; when the lidar scan regularly crosses the land-water interface.

Load the bathymetry settings by selecting *Load Bathymetry Settings* from the *Load* menu in the *Process EAARL Data* window. The *bathctl* window will open (fig. 14) with a list of variables (table 5).

Table 5. Submerged topography settings.

Feature	Functionality
Laser	Estimates exponential decay. The value is represented by the magenta line.
Water	Represents the exponential decay over the water column. The value is represented by the gray exponential curve.
AGC	Is the exponential equalizer. The value is represented by the magenta line.
Thresh	Represents a threshold number. The value above this number will be a "good" return and below this value will be considered noise. This value is represented by a red straight line that connects first and last lines.
First	The algorithm begins looking for a first surface return at this value. The value is represented by the left-hand green line.
Last	The algorithm stops looking for a bottom return at this value. The value is represented by the right-hand red line.
Max. Sat	This value represents the maximum saturation of a return that is acceptable.

Click the *Process Now* button. The user will observe the *Flight Segment Progress Bar* while the command window will list the details of the submerged topography data processing. A return [>] will appear when the submerged topography data processing has finished. Go to the *Process EAARL Data* window to view the processed data. Choose *depth_all* from the *Variable* drop-down menu. Choose *Submerged Topography* from the *Mode* drop-down menu. Do not change the *in Win* menu. Click the *Auto Fma* button to refresh the plot window each time a plot is complete. Click the *Histogram Elevations* button. Select the *Both* button on the *Color Bar Tool*. Click the locations on the histogram that correspond to the minimum [*Cmin*] and maximum [*Cmax*] elevations. Click *Plot* and a window will open with a view of the processed data. These data are unfiltered, so noise may be visible. Elevations higher

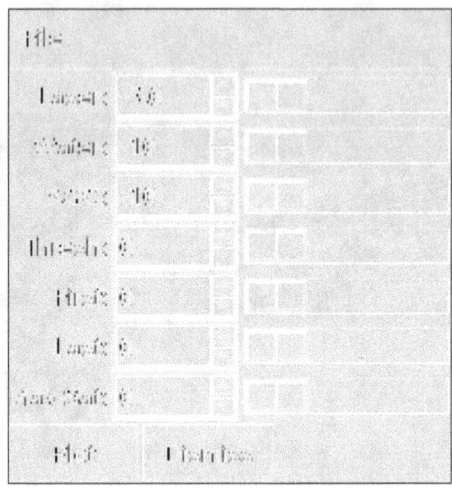

Figure 14. Submerged topography settings window.

than *Cmax* will appear white, while elevations lower than *Cmin* will not appear.

To link the processed submerged topography data with the waveforms, raster images, and RGB images, go to the *Options* menu on the *Process EAARL Data* window. Select the *Show raw and processed waveforms when using Pixel Waveform*. Press the *Pixel Waveform* button. Left click on the data window to examine a point, center click to set as a reference point, and right click to quit the pixel waveform module. When left clicking over the data points, three windows will open. One will display the raw submerged topography waveform for that data point (fig. 15), one will show the processed waveform, and a third window will display the raster image.

The sample raw waveform window in figure 15 represents a shallow, submerged topography region. The waveform window in figure 15 is showing the selection of the bottom return.

Each of the controlling variables is listed in figure 14. If the variables are changed to such a degree that a bottom return is not selected, the terminal window and the raw waveform window will state the reason the bottom was not selected (*Below threshold*). Every time a variable is altered, the alteration is saved by ALPS, and final settings will be applied to all of the submerged topography processing.

Determining the Roll Bias

System installation angles, aircraft orientation angles, and the resulting beam angle are examples of calibration parameters set up for each lidar system (fig. 16). These dimensions usually remain stable; however, over time or whenever the system is removed from the surveying platform, the biases can change significantly. Knowing these parameters on a flight-by-flight basis is important because erroneous values can result in users misinterpreting data as a "signal" instead of noise (Shrestha and others, 2007).

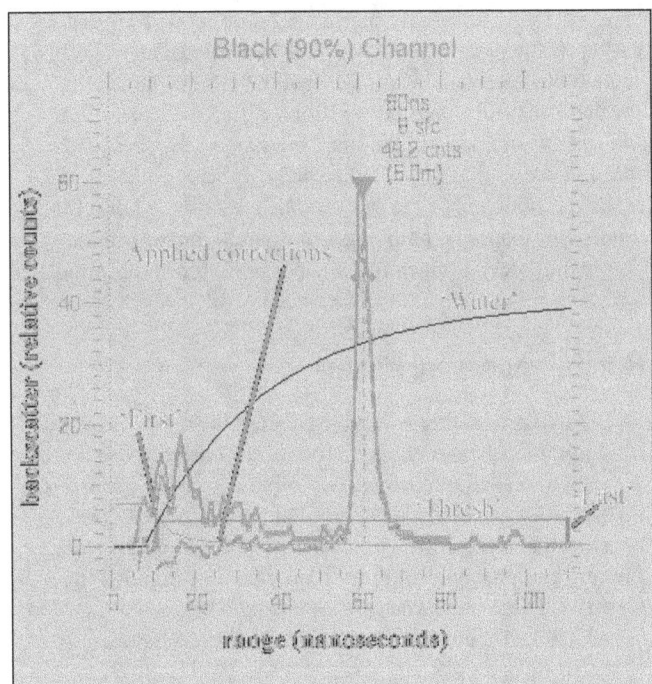

Figure 15. Submerged topography waveform display with the raw waveform (black) and the processed waveform (blue) after the submerged topography settings are applied.

All of the mission constants are set up in the *ops_conf.i* file. The only constant that is usually adjusted is the roll bias. To determine the constant values, either type in the command line **ops_conf** or go to the *Current Ops_conf Settings* submenu within the *Settings* menu in the *Current Data* window (fig. 16).

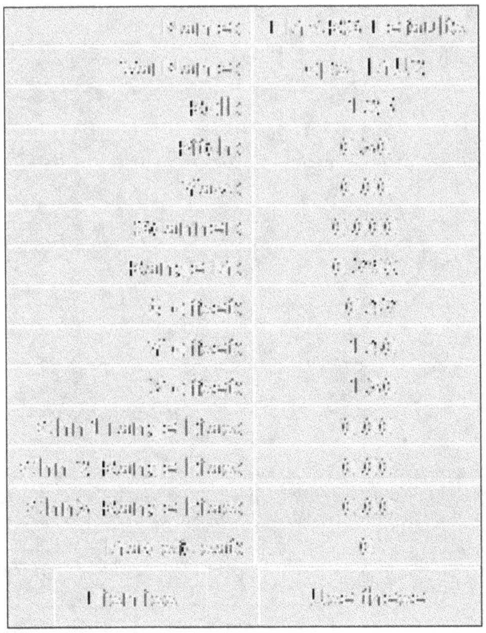

Figure 16. The ops_conf settings window.

There should be a different roll bias for each day, so a different *ops_conf* file should be placed in each mission day's folder. Review the following steps to determine the proper roll bias constant for the applicable mission day.

If not already completed, begin loading the data by repeating the steps in Opening ALPS Processing Windows, Loading the EAARL Database File, Loading GPS Flight Track Information, Loading DMARS Information, and Loading Mission Constants sections of this manual. Zoom in to a small area of the loaded flight lines in the *Yorick 6* window. For determining the roll bias, the user should focus on areas where overlapping flight lines exist. Those flown over an airport runway or parking lot are ideal candidates for analysis. It is possible to analyze the data over features with variable slopes (sand dunes), but data from flat slopes will result in a more accurate determination of the roll bias. To find a flat area, the user may want to load the flight lines (.kml/ kmz files) in Google Earth.

If the *Process EAARL Data* window is not open, go to the *eaarl* window and select *Lidar >> Process Lidar Data* directory. Select an area of flight lines to process by going in the *Define Region* drop-down menu on the *Process EAARL Data* window. (See Topographic Lidar Data Processing for reference.) Select one of the following tools:

- Points in Polygon

- Rubberband Box

- Rectangular Coords

Once a tool is chosen, a window will open discussing the selection. If the *Points in Polygon* tool was selected, draw a polygon over the flight lines. If processing for sub-aerial topography elevations, select *Topo Under Veg* in the drop-down menu located next to the *Define Region* drop-down menu. Choose *Submerged Topography* if processing for bathymetric elevations. It is not necessary to use the *Method* drop-down menu or the *in Win:* menu. Click on *Process Now* and wait until the > appears in the command prompt, indicating that the processing has finished.

To view the processed data, select the *Variable* as *veg_all* or *depth_all* for sub-aerial topography or submerged topography, respectively. Select the *Mode* as *Bare Earth Topography* or *Submerged Topography*. Do not change *in Win* menu in the *Process EAARL Data* window. Click on the *Auto Fma* button to refresh the screen after each plot. Click the *Histogram Elevations* button and select the *Both* button to determine the maximum elevation, *Cmax*, and the minimum elevation, *Cmin*, to be displayed. Click *Plot* to display the processed data.

To evaluate the roll bias, use the *mtransect* command. This command will be used to view a two-dimensional slice of the elevation data by creating a graph of all of the points located within 1.5 m of the drawn line. Type in the command line **info, mtransect** or go to the *CmdLine* menu in the *Process EAARL Data* window and select *mtransect*. A window will open in which instructions for usage of the function and descriptions of function inputs are displayed. In the command line, type the following:

mtransect, variable to process, iwin=input, owin=output, xfma=1, rtn= [1-veg last return and 2-submerged topo], **show=1** [press *enter*]. For example, **mtransect, veg_all, iwin=5, owin=4, xfma=1, rtn=1, show=1** [press *enter*]. Use only **rtn=1** and **veg_all** as the variable to process on last return topography data. Use **rtn=2** and **depth_all** as the variable to process when performing roll bias analysis on submerged topography data. The *mtransect* command is intended for last return or submerged topography data.

Draw a line in the input data window by left clicking the mouse and dragging across the plotted data. Release the mouse to view the output window, which displays elevation data from separate flight lines as different colors. In the output window, zoom in to the overlapping areas until the y-axis has 0.5-m intervals. The difference in elevation between the flight lines should be <0.5 m (fig. 17). Another problem that can be encountered is a dip down or a dip up in overlapping sections (this would appear as an X on the output screen). In this case, try lowering the elevation difference between the flight lines by changing the roll bias value. This can be done by typing **ops_conf.roll_bias=#** [for example, **ops_conf.roll_bias=-1.22**] into the command line.

Every time a new roll bias is entered, the data will have to be reprocessed. Note that these changes are only temporary and will only be made permanent when the *ops_conf* file is changed by using editors such as gedit or kedit. To process and view the data with the new roll bias, repeat steps in this section. To determine if the new roll bias was a better fit for the data, reevaluate the elevation differences using the *mtransect* command in the same location as the previous *mtransect* command. Once the final roll bias is determined, make the final edit to the *ops_conf* file by typing **kedit file name**. [for example, **kedit ops_conf_multi_base.i**] in the command line. At this point, it is possible to batch process the data.

Batch Processing Mode

Batch processing is used to process the entire flight path for a given mission day. This process automatically sections the data into 2-kilometer (km) by 2-km data tiles. In the 2-km by 2-km tiling scheme, data are tiled based on the UTM coordinates of the northwest corner. The 2-km by 2-km data tiles are further organized into 10-km by 10-km index tiles (fig. 18). These index tiles are also named based on the UTM coordinates of the northwest corner. Data tiles are named as *t_eXXX000_nXXXX000_XX*. The *eXXXX000* is the easting of the northwest corner and the *nXXXX000* is the northing of the northwest corner. The attached XX to the file name is the UTM zone for the tile. Index tiles are named similarly but begin with "i" instead of "t", thus *i_eXXX000_nXXXX000_XX* (*i_e451000_n4240000_18* for the index tile and *t_e454000_n4242000_18* for the date tile). The batch processing mode

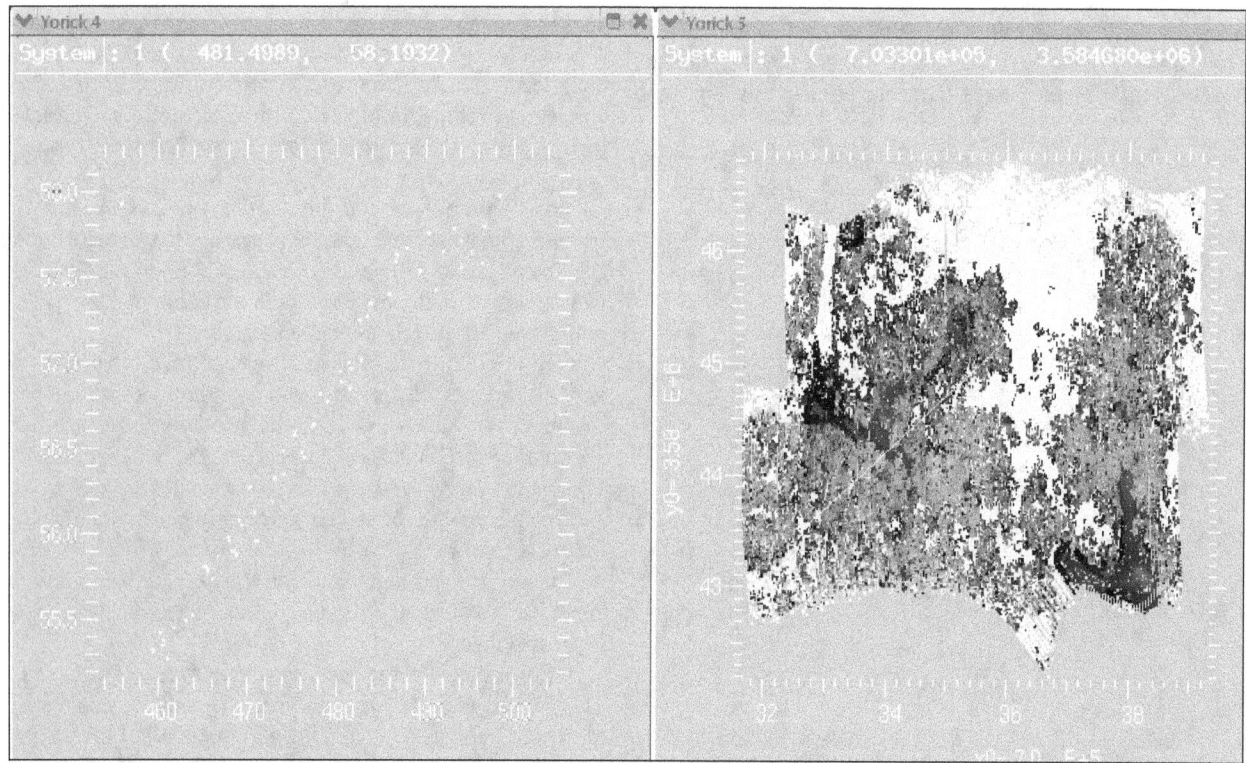

Figure 17. The panel on the right shows elevation data from overlapping flight lines. A vertical transect (represented by the red line) through the data is shown on the panel on the left. Each color represents a flight line.

can only be performed after all of the mission data are loaded and the roll bias has been determined for the flight day via interactively processing small segments of the flight path. (See the Interactive Processing Mode sections.)

Begin the batch processing by typing **help, batch_process** into the command line. Alternatively, select *batch_process* within the *CmdLine* drop-down menu on the *Process EAARL Data* window. This will open a help document about what parameters to include in the batch processing command (table 6). Set the UTM zone number by typing **curzone=#** [for example, **curzone=16**] in the command line. Once the parameters are determined, enter the following command in the command line: **batch_process, typ=, save_dir="", zone=, mdate="", pick=, update=** [press *enter*]. For example, **batch_process, typ=1, save_dir="/training/katrina/Index_Tiles/", zone=16, mdate="20050908", pick=1** [press *enter*].

After the command, which includes **pick=1**, has been entered, the prompt will state the following: *Hold the left mouse button down, select a region*. If **pick=2**, the prompt will state: *Left mouse generates a vertice. Ctl-Left or middle mouse click to end and close polygon*. Go to the *Yorick 6* window (displayed flight lines) and select the area to process.

Green boxes will appear over the flight lines; these represent the 2-km by 2-km data tiles into which the data will be separated. The command window will run through the batch-processing sequence. The command window will list the

details of processing, and the data tiles will turn black on the screen after the processing has finished (fig. 19). A return [>] will also appear at the command line. This process may take up to a day to complete, depending upon the amount of data processed. This, in turn, depends on the size of the selected area. It is best to initiate this process at the end of the day so that it will run overnight. The batch_process command only has to be executed only once per mission day; the user will have to batch process the data only once for first and last return topography. The separation of the data into bare earth and first return occurs during the filtering step.

Filtering

ALPS applies statistical filtering methods to remove false bottom returns and other outliers from the EAARL lidar data. Erroneous (outlier) points might include reflections from objects such as birds, multiple atmospheric effects (dust, moisture), or multiple reflections from bright targets. Two filtering methods within ALPS are used to extract ground (bare earth) elevations from a point cloud of processed last returns. These methods are the Random Consensus Filter (RCF) and the Iterative Random Consensus Filter (IRCF). The RCF is the faster and most basic filter in ALPS. The IRCF is a

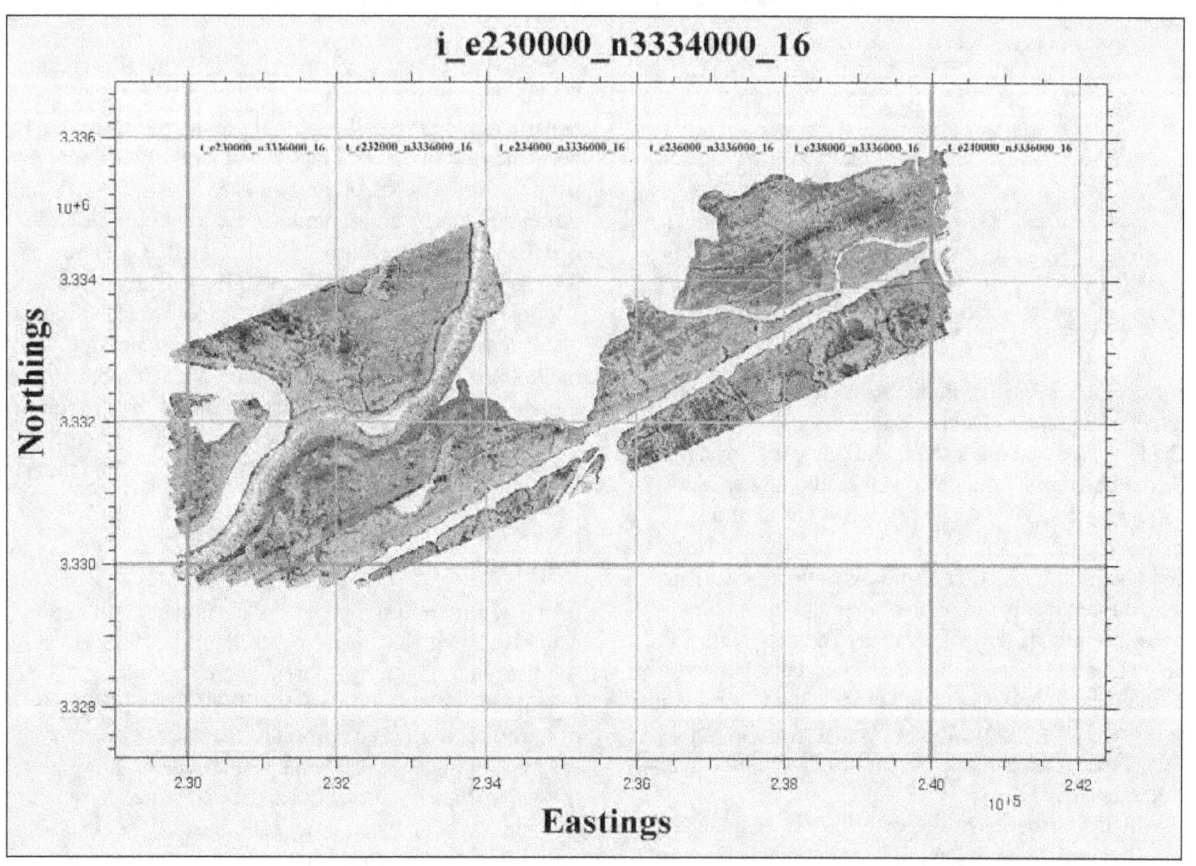

Figure 18. The 2-km by 2-km data tiles are highlighted in pink and the 10-km by 10-km index tiles are highlighted in purple.

Table 6. Batch processing parameters.

Feature	Functionality
typ	Processes data type. For example, 1 for bathymetry and 2 for vegetation (this includes first and last returns).
save_dir=""	Where the files are to be written. Create an Index_Tiles directory (enter in the command line: **mkdir Index_Tiles**). The index and data tile files will go inside of this directory [for example, **save_dir="/training/katrina/Index_Tiles/"**].
zone	Sets the UTM zone number [for example, **zone=16**].
mdate=""	Is the date the mission was flown in a yyyymmdd format [**mdate="20050908"**].
onlyplot	Set to 1 to plot data. This function will not process data. This function will plot boxes around the data tiles that are to be processed.
pbd or edf	Writes out the files to either a .pbd (default) or .edf format. Select only one output format.
win	Designates the location of the flight line information. The default for this function is 6. This will not be changed unless the users changes the flight line window.
pick	Set equal to 1 to use the rubberband box selection method or to 2 to use the points in a polygon selection method.
update	Set to 1 to process files that have not been processed. This function will not affect already processed files.
avg_surf	Set to 1 to use the average water surface reflections when processing for bathymetry. The default for this parameter is avg_surf=1. Set to 0 to disable this function. Set this variable to 0 when the use Fresnel reflections to determine water surface has been unselected.

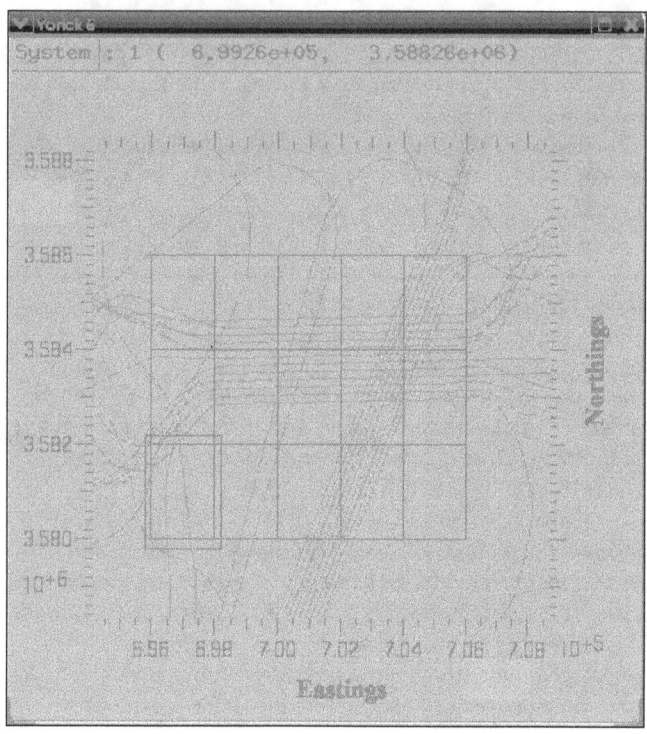

Figure 19. Highlighted in green are the flight lines selected to process in batch processing mode. As the flight lines are processed, they are highlighted in black.

A triangulated irregular network (TIN) model is created from the labeled ground points. The TIN model is continuously densified by adding all potential ground points within the vertical width for each triangulated facet. The points rejected from the first RANSAC iteration are treated as potential ground points. Each triangulated facet within the TIN model is defined as a three-dimensional plane, the equation of which is determined from the vertices of the triangulated facet. All potential ground points above or below each facet are classified as ground if they fall within the user-defined vertical range (also called the TIN elevation width) from the three-dimensional plane. The process continues for a predefined number of iterations or when less than 2% of potential ground points are added to the final set of ground elevations (Nayegandhi and others, 2009).

Random Consensus Filtering

The first return topography data must be filtered using RCF, which can also be used to filter last returns and submerged topography returns where appropriate. The RCF function can be used to test the filter parameters on the dataset or to refilter a specific portion of the dataset after a batch filter has been applied. (See Manual Filtering/Editing section.) The following filtering protocol can be performed only after each mission has been batch processed. See the previous section on Batch Processing Mode for completing these steps.

slower process, because it combines several RCF passes with an iterative triangulation technique.

The RCF is based on the Random Sample Consensus (RANSAC) paradigm, which was originally published by Fischler and Bolles (1981). The filter uses a grid of non-overlapping square cells of user-defined size overlaid onto the original point cloud. The user also defines the grid cell size and vertical tolerance based on the topographic complexity and point-sampling density of the data. The maximum allowable elevation range within a cell is established by the vertical tolerance (Nayegandhi and others, 2004). An iterative process searches for the maximum concentration of points within the vertical tolerance and removes those points outside of the tolerance (fig. 20).

For the IRCF, the RANSAC paradigm is used to determine the initial point cloud that represents the ground.

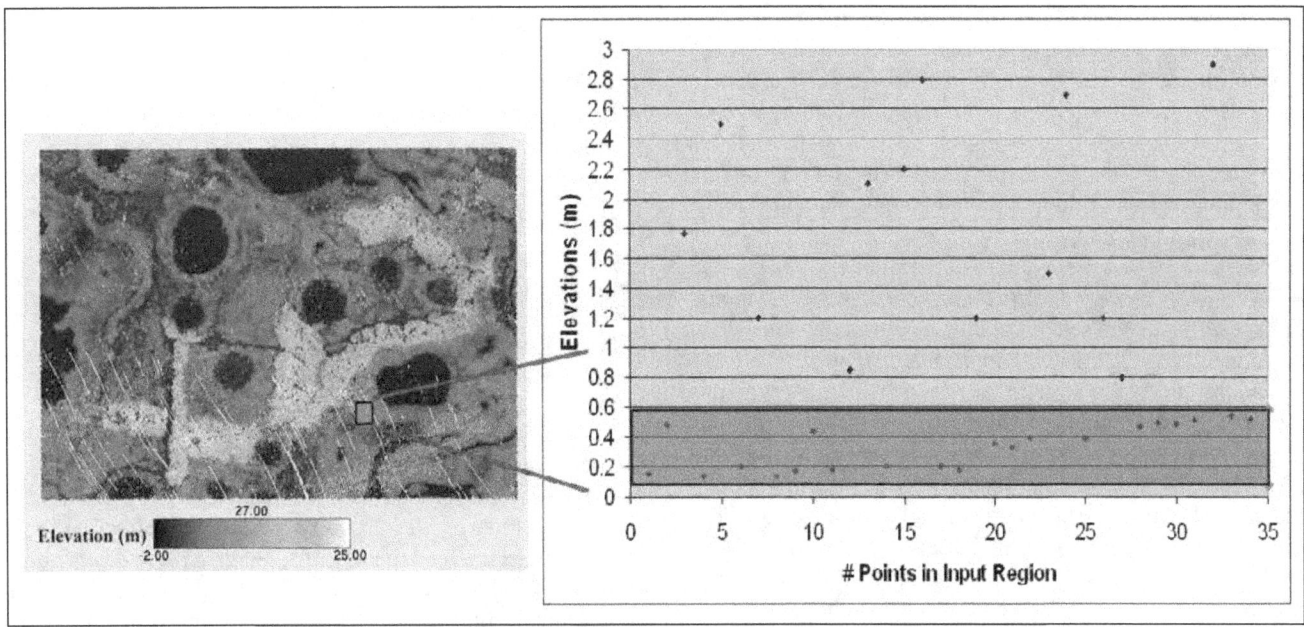

Figure 20. The image on the right shows a vertical slice of data from the image on the left. The image on the right shows a concentration of points on the ground and several outliers. The data outside of the red rectangle highlight the points that would be removed (Nayegandhi and others, 2004).

Interactive RCF

Go to the *PostProcessing* menu in the *Process EAARL Data* window and select RCF *Region Filter*. The *Random Consensus Filter* window will open (fig. 21). In the *Select RCF type* drop-down menu, select *RCF*. The *Input Window (cm)* default value is 500 centimeter (cm) and the *Elevation width (cm)* default value is 20 cm. For the buffer [*Input Window*], choose a value around 600 or higher. This value would partition all of the points into 6-m by 6-m squares. This value should decrease to account for increasing sloping regions. The input window also depends on the data density. Select a smaller window size if the density is high. The tolerance or vertical window [*Elevation Width*] should be a value of around 400 or higher for first return topography. If using this RCF for last return topography, the value should be around 20 to 40 cm for relatively flat surfaces, and 40 to 100 cm for sloping surfaces. If the analyst has prior knowledge of the mapped region, select the tolerance value to be the maximum range of elevation expected within the input window. Set *Minimum*

winners to 3. The *Input Variable* takes the loaded variable from the *Process EAARL Data* window. Make sure the correct tile is being filtered. The *Mode* should be changed to whatever mode is being viewed. This *Mode* will be the same as the *Mode* on the *Process EAARL Data* menu. The *Output Variable* will already be created and *rcf_* will be inserted to the beginning of the *Input Variable* name [for example, *Input Variable*: *bet_20070912_6* and *Output Variable*: *rcf_bet_20070912_6*]. Click the *Go* button; the RCF function will start to process. The command terminal will display a return [>] when the filtering has been completed.

To view the filtered data, go to the *Process EAARL Data* window and choose a different *in Win:* for the data to display. Select the new variable [for example, *rcf_bet_20070912_6*] by clicking the *Variable* drop-down menu and click *Plot* to view the newly filtered data. If these are the desired parameters with which to RCF filter the data, then run the batch filter for the remaining data. (See Batch Filtering section of this manual for instructions.)

Iterative Random Consensus Filtering

The IRCF is used to filter last returns and submerged topography returns. If utilized in the interactive mode, IRCF can be used manually to edit erroneous elevations in the dataset by deleting triangles from the TIN surface. This meticulous process focuses on the final elevation points consistent with bare earth and submerged topography.

The IRCF parameters (fig. 22), without the interactive functions, are similar to those used with the RCF function. The

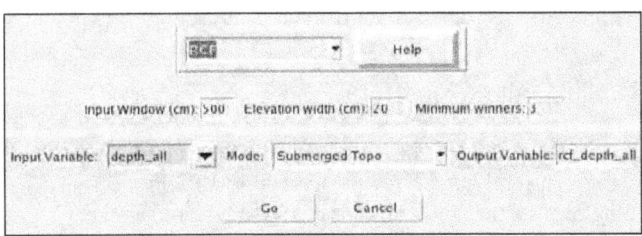

Figure 21. The Random Consensus Filter window.

only difference is that additional parameters such as minimum and maximum *Pre-filter Elevations (m)*, *TIN elev width (cm)*, *Plot TIN in win*, and the *Distance Threshold (m)* can be set or changed to affect the iterative process. *Input Window* should be a value of about 500 cm or higher. The *Elevation width (cm)* should be about 20 to 40 cm for flat surfaces and 30 to 80 cm for sloping surfaces. Submerged topography should be treated similar to last return topography when determining filtering parameters.

From the *Process EAARL Data* window, select *Random Consensus Filter* and select *Iterative RCF* from the drop-down menu (fig. 22). The minimum and maximum *Pre-filter Elevations (m)* should be set if the analyst is familiar with the elevation range within that study area. The *Tin elev width (cm)* should be set to 20 to 30 cm for relatively flat areas and 20 to 60 cm for sloping areas. Set *Minimum winners* as 3. The *Input Variable* takes the loaded variable from the *Process EAARL Data* window. The *Mode* should be changed to whatever mode is being viewed. The *Output Variable* will already be created and *rcf_* will be inserted into the beginning of the *Input Variable* name. Click the *Go* button; the filter will begin processing. The command terminal will display a return [>] when the processing has been completed.

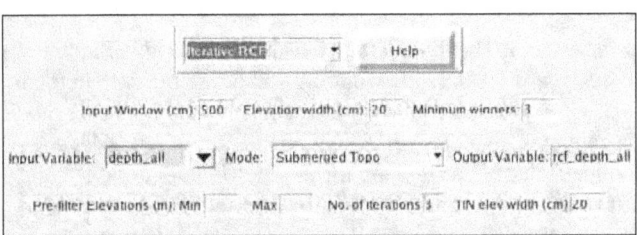

Figure 22. The Iterative Random Consensus Filter window.

Interactive IRCF

To use the Interactive IRCF, repeat steps from the IRCF section above. Click the *Interactive?* button and click *Go*. The IRCF filter will run and a new window will open with gridded data. Zoom in on the triangles with erroneous data that need to be deleted. The command prompt will read *Interactive Mode? (yes/no/done/end)*. Enter **yes** in the command line. *Click left to continue selection, middle to pan/zoom, right to select similar; CTRL-Right=End Interactive Mode or CTRL-left=Retriangulate.* Select similar triangles to delete, then control-left to retriangulate the area. The prompt will then ask to continue interactive mode. Typing **no** or **done** on the command line will put the area through a series of iterations while allowing the user to select triangles for further deletion. Continue repeating the above steps until the entire area is ready to be retriangulated; type **end** to finish the iterations.

To view the filtered data, go to the *Process EAARL Data* window and choose the filtered data to plot. The new variable should already be loaded in the list. Select the *rcf_* variable

[for example, *rcf_bet_20070912_6*] and click *Plot* to view the newly processed data. If these are the desired parameters with which to IRCF filter the data, then run the batch filter for the remaining data. (See Batch Filtering section of this manual for instructions.)

Batch Filtering

Like batch processing, batch filtering saves valuable time by eliminating the effort required to interactively filter the lidar data. Additional erroneous data can be removed during the manual editing session after batch filtering has been completed. (See Manual Filtering/Editing section.)

If the windows: *ytk*, *eaarl*, and *Process EAARL Data* are not currently open, see the Opening ALPS Processing Windows section for instruction. Opening these windows will load a series of files that are necessary for batch filtering. The user need not load the day of flight data [*pnav*, *dmars*, or *ops_conf* files] that were required for the interactive and batch processing detailed in the Processing of Raw EAARL Data section of this manual.

In the command line, type **help, batch_rcf** or select from the *Process EAARL Data* window *CmdLine >> batch_rcf(Filter)*. A window will open in which instructions for usage of the batch filtering function and descriptions of function inputs are displayed (table 7). Set the UTM zone number by typing **curzone=#** [for example, **curzone=16**] in the command line. Once the user has determined the parameters needed to batch filter, type the following command: **batch_rcf, "directory", buf=, w=, mode=, meta=, write_merge=, rcfmode=, searchstr=""** [press *enter*]. For example, **batch_rcf, "/training/katrina/Index_Tiles/", buf=600, w=400, mode=1, meta=1, write_merge=1, rcfmode=1, searchstr="*_v.pbd"** [press *enter*].

This batch filtering process can take anywhere from a few hours for the RCF to a couple of days for the IRCF; it also depends on the amount of data that are being filtered. Once the function has finished, the user will see a return [>] at the command prompt.

Image Plots

ALPS includes utilities to generate image plots with the processed and filtered EAARL data. Viewing the plots confirms that the appropriate mission constants and filter parameters were applied for the survey area.

Loading Image Plot Data

If the windows *ytk*, *eaarl*, and *Process EAARL Data* are not currently open, see the Opening ALPS Processing Windows section for instruction. To load data for image generation, select the *Read Data Directory* option within the *File* menu in the *Process EAARL Data* window. The *Read Data*

Table 7. Batch filtering parameters.

Feature	Functionality
"directory"	Is the directory name within which all the files are processed [for example, **"/training/katrina/ Index_Tiles/"**].
buf	Is the horizontal size in centimeters of the area to be filtered (default is 700 cm).
w	Is the vertical height in centimeters (default is 200 cm).
mode	The type of data to be filtered. Set to 1 for first return, 2 for submerged topography, and 3 for ground under vegetation (bare earth).
meta	Set to 1 for the RCF parameters to include the file name.
write_merge	Set to 1 to have the files merged before filtering. This parameter is useful when using the manual editing replace function. See the section on Manual Filtering/Editing for details on the replace function.
rcfmode	Sets the type of filter being applied to data. Set to a value of 2 for the iterative RCF (IRCF filter for bare earth and submerged topography only), 1 for the plain RCF filter, and 0 to disable the filter (use when doing a merge only). The default value for this parameter is 2.
searchstr=""	Searches for these files to process [for example, **searchstr="*_v.pbd"**].
update	Set this to 1 to process only those files that have not yet been filtered. This will not affect already filtered files.

Directory window will open. In the window, click the *Browse* button to navigate to the directory with the index tiles. Select one of the index tiles that includes data. In *Data Type*, select *.pbd*. *Search String* defines the type of files to be loaded. Type ***_v.pbd** to load processed, unfiltered last return and first return data, ***_b.pbd** to load processed, unfiltered submerged topography data, and ***fs*rcf*.pbd** as an example to load the first return processed, filtered data. In the *Merged Variable*, specify a variable name for the data. Use a variable name that will be easy to remember and that reflects that type of data loaded [for example, *fs_rcf_merge*]. Click the *Unique* button to load only one of the overlapping points from each data tile. Choose a *Subsample* number. A number between 10 and 50 is a good range of values for viewing 2 to 10 data tiles, but the numbers will depend on the size of the area being plotted and the point density. The data may overlap UTM zones. To view a particular UTM zone, click on the *Fixed Zone* button. Select the *Zone* number and select whether the data is in *2k Data Tiles* or *Quarter Quads*. (See Quarter Quadrangle Description section.) Click *Load Data*.

Viewing Image Plot Data

To view the loaded data, make sure the variable with the loaded data was added to the variable list. Click the *Variable* button on the *Process EAARL Data* window. This will open the *List* window. In the *List* window, click on the merged variable name in the list and click the *Select* button, or go to the *Process EAARL Data* window and use the *Variable* drop-down menu to select the merged variable name. If the variable name is not in the list, enter it into the *List* window and click *Add*; click the *Select* button to select the variable. Confirm the *Mode* is appropriate whether it is the *First Return Topography*, *Bare Earth Topography*, or *Submerged Topography*. Change *in Win:* to another number in order to have this data plot in another window. Select the *Histogram Elevations* button to determine the maximum elevation, *Cmax*, and the minimum elevation, *Cmin*, to display. To change the graph size, go to the *Graph* menu in the *Process Eaarl Data* window and select the *100 Dpi (1100x850)* to be able to plot the largest size graph. Always confirm that the *Auto Fma* button is depressed to refresh the plot with subsequent changes made to the graph. Click *Plot*. Repeat steps for other types of data.

Saving Image Plots

Finally, save an image of the plotted data (figs. 23 and 24). First make sure the image to be saved is the current window specified in *in Win:* in the *Process Eaarl Data window*. Next, add a color bar, which defines the minimum and maximum elevation values shown in the plot. Click the *Color Bar* button. Left click and drag into the window with the loaded data. Select an area where the color bar will be displayed. Create a plot title by typing **pltitle ("Title")** on the command line. The title will appear at the top of the loaded data window (figs. 23 and 24); **pltitle ("Before IRCF")**.

To save this image, go to the *Imagery* menu in the *eaarl* window and select *Capture a display*. A window will open with the following instructions: *Raise the window you want to capture, click OK, and then click on the desired window*. Click *OK* on the instructional window and click on the window to be captured. A *Save As* window will open. Navigate to an appropriate directory in which to save the image and click *Save*. This will automatically save the image as a .png file.

Datum Conversion

ALPS includes utilities for projecting the data to other datums so that the dataset can be compared with other existing datasets. Geodetic datums represent the size and shape of the Earth and the origin and orientation of the coordinate systems. Datums have evolved over time from those describing a spherical Earth to ellipsoidal models derived from satellite measurements. Datum changes require a periodic update due

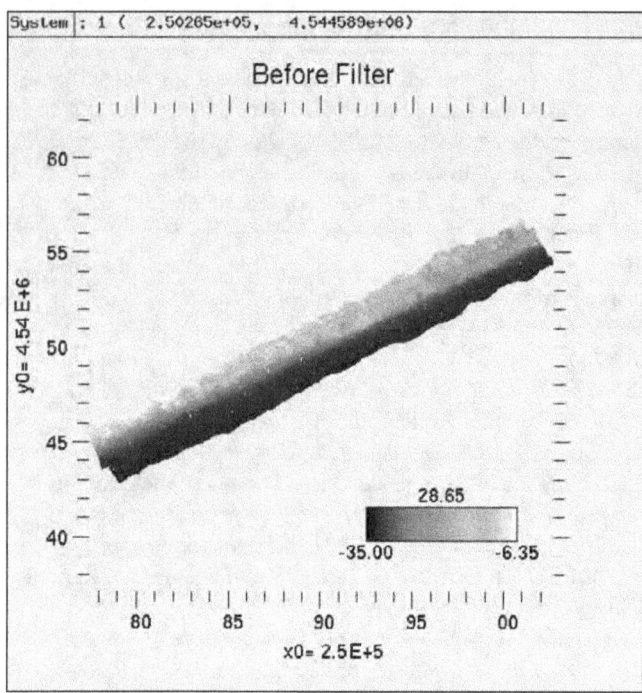

Figure 23. Image plot showing unfiltered elevation data from -35 m to -6.35 m. Elevation values are in WGS84 ellipsoid heights. The yellow specks represent noise that filtering would help remove.

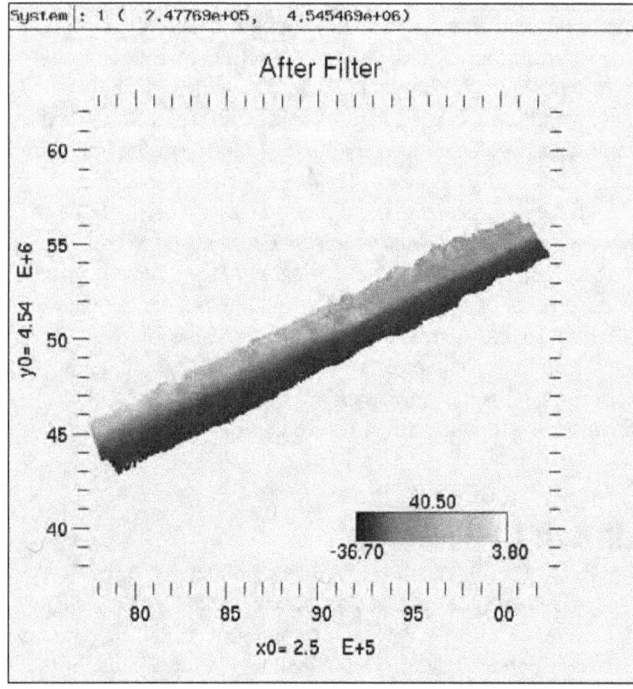

Figure 24. Image plot showing filtered elevation data from -36.70 m to -3.80 m. Elevations values are in WGS84 ellipsoid heights. The yellow specks have mostly been filtered out.

to changes in the geologic structure of the Earth's surface, such as subsidence, uplift, and sea-level change. ALPS can convert the ellipsoid heights (WGS84 G1150) to orthometric heights (NAD83, NAVD88) using the GEOID03 model. This is an important process because each datum transformation can introduce a 1- to 5-cm error into the data with each datum transformation (Nayegandhi and others, 2006).

Datum conversions occur in the batch mode and the process generates a new *.pbd* file with *_n88* in the file name. If the windows *ytk*, *eaarl*, and *Process EAARL Data* are not currently open, see the Opening ALPS Processing Windows section for instructions. Opening these windows will load a series of files that are necessary for batch datum conversion to begin. Set the curzone/utmzone [for example, **curzone=16** or **utmzone=16**]. Type **help, batch_datum_convert** in the command line. Alternatively, select *batch_datum_convert* within the *CmdLine* menu in the *Process EAARL Data* window. This will open a help document about the parameters to include in the batch datum conversion command (table 8). Type the following command: **batch_datum_convert, "directory", zone_nbr=, searchstr=""** [press *enter*]. For example, **batch_datum_convert, "/training/katrina/Index_Tiles/", zone_nbr=16, searchstr="*merged_rcf.pbd"** [press *enter*].

Datum conversions can take a couple of hours or less to complete, depending on the data size. Once the function has finished, a return [>] will appear in the command prompt.

Table 8. Batch datum conversion parameters.

Feature	Functionality
"directory"	The directory name within which the files are processed [for example, **"/training/katrina/Index_Tiles/"**].
zone_nbr	Sets the UTM zone number.
searchstr=""	Sets the search string instead of using rcfmode [for example, **searchstr="*ircf*.pbd"**].
tonad83	Set to 0 to not use this conversion. Otherwise converts files to NAD 83 reference datum.
tonavd88	Set to 0 if the user does not want to utilize this command. Otherwise converts files to NAVD 88 reference datum.
rcfmode	Set to 1 to convert RCF'd files and set to 2 to convert IRCF'd files. This option is replaced by using the search string.
geoid_version	Set to "GEOID99" to use the GEOID99 model or "GEOID96" to use the GEOID96 model. Otherwise, the default is the GEOID03 model.
update	Set to 1 to process only those files that have not yet been converted. This will not affect already converted files.

Quarter Quadrangle

The quarter quadrangle (QQ) tiling scheme is commonly used for organizing digital orthoimagery. Airborne Topographic Mapper (ATM) (Airborne Topographic Mapper Data Processing section) or some sizeable EAARL datasets are organized in this way. This tiling scheme is used for lidar data dissemination by the U.S. Geological Survey (USGS) Center for Lidar Information Coordination and Knowledge (CLICK). Furthermore, this tiling scheme facilitates lidar and orthoimagery comparisons, which can be an important component of lidar quality assurance and control.

Quarter Quadrangle Description

In the QQ tiling scheme, each tile is 1/16 of a degree (3.75 minutes) in width and height. The tiles are named by referencing their southeast corners, with boundaries on every 1/16 of a degree latitude and longitude of the NAD83 datum. The naming scheme uses a structure of AAOOOOaoq (table 9). For example, 47104h2c means:

47   47 degrees north latitude
104   104 degrees west longitude
h   is 8th in sequence, so it is the last section and starts at 7/8 of a degree, or 0.875
2   2 is second in sequence, so it is in the 2nd section and would start at 1/8 of a degree, or 0.125
c   this designates the northwest corner, which means we add 1/16 of a degree to both the north and west, or 0.0625 to each.

47104 is the square degree designated at 47° N., 104° W. The h2 describes the quadrangle with a southeast corner at 47.875° N., 104.125° W. The c indicates it is the QQ with a southeast corner at 47.9375° N., 104.1875° W.

ALPS 2-km to Quarter Quadrangle Conversion

To convert ATM (Airborne Topographic Mapper Data Processing section) or EAARL data into the QQ format, type **help, batch_2k_to_qq** in the command line. This opens a help document about parameters to include in the batch QQ conversion (table 10). Type in the command line in this specific order: **batch_2k_to_qq, "src_dir", "dest_dir", mode, searchstr="", dir_struc=1, buffer=30** [press *enter*]. For example: **batch_2k_to_qq, "/training/katrina/Index_Tiles/", "/training/katrina/be_QQ_tiles/", 3, searchstr="*n88*ircf*_mf.pbd", dir_struc=1, buffer=30** [press *enter*].

Quarter Quadrangle to ALPS 2-km Conversion

To convert the ATM (Airborne Topographic Mapper Data Processing section) or EAARL data into the 2-km format, type in the command line: **help, batch_qq_to_2k**. This opens

Table 9. Quarter quadrangle tiling scheme.

Character Representation	Character Type	Designation
AA	Positive whole number.	Degrees latitude.
000	Positive whole number. Value is zero padded to a width of three numbers, if necessary.	Degrees longitude.
a	Alpha character.	Characters a-h designate which quadrangle in the degree of latitude, where a is the closest to zero minutes and h is the closest to the next full degree. Each character represents 1/8th of a degree.
o	Numeral	Numbers 1-8 designate the quadrangle in the degree of longitude, where 1 is closest to zero minutes and 8 is closest to the next full degree. Each numeral represents 1/8 of a degree.
q	Alpha character.	Characters a-d designate the quarter in the quadrangle, where a is the southeast quarter, b is the northeast corner, c is the northwest corner, and d is the southwest corner. Each quarter quadrant is 1/16 of a degree in latitude and 1/16 of a degree in longitude.

a help document regarding which parameters to include in the batch conversion (table 11). Type in the command line in this specific order: **batch_qq_to_2k, "src_dir", "dest_dir", mode, searchstr="", buffer=30** [press *enter*]. For example: **batch_qq_to_2k, "/training/katrina/Index_Tiles/", "/training/katrina/be_QQ_tiles/", 3, searchstr="*n88*ircf*_mf.pbd", buffer=30** [press *enter*].

Table 10. Quarter Quadrangle to ALPS 2-km conversion parameters.

Feature	Functionality
"src_dir"	Designates the location of the source directory. It should be the directory structure containing the EAARL 2-km x 2-km tiles in .pbd format.
"dest_dir"	Designates the directory that the quarter quadrangle .pbd would go into.
mode	The type of EAARL that will be converted. Use only the number to represent the type of data. Set the values equal to 1 for first return, 2 for bathymetry, and 3 for bare earth.
searchstr=""	Searches for these files to process [for example, **searchstr="*n88*ircf*_mf.pbd"**].
dir_struc	Set equal to 1 to create a quarter quadrangle directory structure similar to the index tile structure.

Airborne Topographic Mapper Data Processing

The ATM is a single-return, green-wavelength lidar system developed by the National Aeronautic and Space Administration (NASA). The original purpose for this lidar system was to measure the changing Arctic and Antarctic ice caps and glaciers. The ATM has also been employed in observing coastal-morphology change. The ATM system is mounted to a small aircraft that flies around 400 to 800 m AGL (fig. 25). Tested accuracy of the ATM data is about 10 to 20 cm. In 2001, a down-looking camera was added to the ATM lidar system (Harris and others, 2005).

The ATM raw data are stored as binary *.qi* files and contain only first returns. All of the *.qi* files that are intended

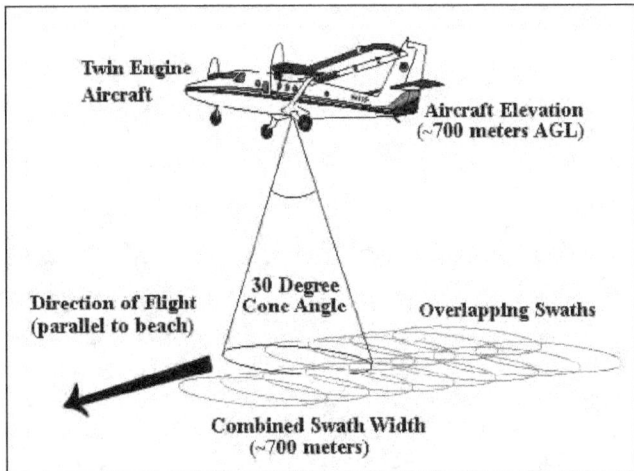

Figure 25. The elliptical scan pattern of the ATM system (Sallenger and Brock, 2001).

Table 11. Quarter Quadrangle to ALPS 2-km conversion parameters.

Feature	Functionality
"src_dir"	The source directory [for example, **"/training/katrina/be_qq/"**]. This should be the root directory that contains the QQ tiles in .pbd format.
"dest_dir"	The destination directory. The index tiles can be written here.
mode	Type of data converted. Use only the number to represent the type of data. Use 1 for first return, 2 for bathymetry, and 3 for bare earth.
searchstr=""	Searches for these files to process [for example, **searchstr="*qq*.pbd"**].
suffix	Inserts a string at the end of each data tile file name. By default, two letters will be inserted based on the mode type. This can include a trailing .pbd. To suppress the suffix, use **suffix=""**.
remove_buffers	Set to 1 to clip each QQ .pbd data to the file's QQ extent. Set to 0 for all of the data to be used, regardless of location. This function defaults to 1.
buffer	Specifies a buffer in meters added around each data tile. Default is buffer=100. Use buffer=0 to suppress the buffer.
uniq	Specifies whether data points should be constrained to only unique points by sod when saved to the pbd file. Default is 1. Set equal to 0 to avoid this constraint. This is necessary with Airborne Topographic Mapper (ATM) data, which may have unreliable sod values.

for processing should be separated by mission date. Multiple mission dates should not be stored in the same directory. Before beginning the ATM processing, open the following windows: *ytk*, *eaarl*, and *Process EAARL Data*. (See the Opening ALPS Processing Windows section for instruction.) conv Opening these windows will load a series of files required for the ATM processing command line scripts. Type **help, batch_qi_to_tiles** in the command line. This will open a help document explaining the parameters to include in the ATM processing command (table 12). The ATM data will be converted into the same index tile and data tile format as is done with the EAARL data. To process the data, type the following command: **batch_qi_to_tiles, "con_dir", ymd, "dir", searchstr="*.qi"**, [press *enter*]. For example:

> **batch_qi_to_tiles,**
> **"/training/qi_data/20011012/", 20011012,**
> **"/training/Index_Tiles/", searchstr="*.qi"** [press *enter*].

Next, merge the data tiles from each mission day by using the *merge_qi_tiles* function. Type **help, merge_qi_tiles** in the

Table 12. Airborne Topographic Mapper processing parameters.

Feature	Functionality
"con_dir"	Sets the directory path of the .qi files to be processed. Separate the .qi files separated by mission date.
ymd	The date the mission was flown in a yyyymmdd format [for example, **20011008**].
"dir"	Sets the output directory organized into the index tile tiling scheme.
searchstr=""	Searches for these files to process [for example, **searchstr="*qi"**].
name	Set this function to append to the beginning of the processed file names.

command line. This will open a help document explaining the parameters to include in the ATM merging command (table 13). To merge the data, type the following command: **merge_qi_tiles, "dir", glob=""** [press *enter*]. For example: **merge_qi_tiles, "/training/Index_Tiles/" glob="*.pbd"** [press *enter*].

Table 13. Airborne Topographic Mapper merging parameters.

Feature	Functionality
"dir"	Sets the directory path of the .qi files to be merged.
glob=""	Searches for these files to process [for example, **glob="*.pbd"**].
srt	If set to 1, data will be sorted by seconds of the epoch before being written to the merged file. This is off by default.

After processing and merging, the ATM data should be converted into the QQ tiling format. See the ALPS 2-km to Quarter Quadrangle Conversion section for the description of this tiling format.

Filtering the ATM data is a separate function from filtering the EAARL data. Type in the command line: **help, rcf_atm_pbds**. The help document that opens outlines the possible parameters for this filtering function (table 14). Type in the command line: **rcf_atm_pbds, "ipath", searchstr="", buf=, w=, meta=1** [press *enter*]. For example: **rcf_atm_pbds, "/training/jboniste/Index_Tiles/", searchstr="*.pbd", buf=2500, w=1200, meta=1** [press *enter*]. This function uses only the rcf filter because ATM data contain only first return topography.

At this point in the processing, if the user wants to convert the data files from ellipsoid heights to orthometric heights, the user must use the *batch_datum_convert* function. The help document can be accessed from the *CmdLine*

Table 14. Airborne Topographic Mapper filtering parameters.

Feature	Functionality
"ipath"	The input directory for the .pbds to be filtered.
ifname=""	Pathname of an individual file that the user wants to filter.
searchstr=""	Searches for the files to process [for example, **searchstr="*n88*.pbd"**].
buf	Sets the horizontal size of the area to be filtered in centimeters.
w	Sets the vertical height of the area in centimeters.
meta	Set to 1 to include the filtering parameters in the file name, otherwise set to 0.
opath=""	Set equal to the output directory for the files. It will default to the same directory as the original .pbd files.

menu on the *Process EAARL Data* window. See the Datum Conversion section of this manual for more details regarding this function.

Once the ATM QQ tiles have been filtered, all remaining functions would operate the same as they would with EAARL data. These functions include manual editing and export as American Standard Code for Information Interchange (ASCII) XYZ or American Society for Photogrammetry and Remote Sensing (ASPRS) Log ASCII Standard (LAS). Refer to the Manual Filtering/Editing, Conversion to ASCII XYZ format, and Conversion to ASPRS LAS format sections of this manual that deal with the editing of point data and product creation.

Manual Filtering/Editing

Several manual editing tools in ALPS remove outliers missed by the batch filtering process and restore valid points. To start the manual editing process, it is usually beneficial to load a boundary area for the data. This is done the same way as loading an image. (See Loading Other Images section of this manual to complete this task.)

If the windows *ytk*, *eaarl*, and *Process EAARL Data* are not currently open, see the Opening ALPS Processing Windows section for instructions. Opening these windows will load a series of files that are necessary for the manual editing of the data to begin.

Manual editing is done by loading each 2-km by 2-km or QQ data tile. Go to the *Process EAARL Data* window>> *File >> Read Binary Data File*. Navigate to the data tiles directory and select one of the filtered *.pbd* files [for example, *t_e575000_n2768000_17_n88_v_b700_w50_n3_merged_ircf.pbd*]. The *Variable* will automatically load. Confirm the *Mode* is appropriate, whether it is the *First Return Topography*, *Bare Earth Topography*, or *Submerged Topography*. Select the *Histogram Elevations* to display the data properly. (See Viewing Processed Topography Data section.) Confirm that distribution of the data is positioned correctly when viewing the histogram (most coastal areas will center near zero). This ensures the datum was properly applied to the data. A larger graph size will allow a better view of the data. To change the graph size, go to the *Graph* menu and select *100 Dpi* to plot a larger graph size (click *Plot*).

UTM Zone Fixing

This function scans through the selected *.pbd* files to ensure the coordinates in each file are properly zoned. Run this function if the collected data cross UTM zones and before completing the Keep/Remove/Elevation Clipper Filter Tools or Replace/Datum-Convert Filter Tools sections. This function will overwrite the *.pbd* files with "corrected" versions of the same file. If there is nothing to fix in a file, the function will not change that file. In the case that a mistake is made, a copy of the data should be created before running the function [for example, **cp –r dir1 dir2**].

To zone fix 2-km data tiles, type in the command line (table 15): **help, batch_fix_dt_zones**. To run the function, type in the command line in this specific order: **batch_fix_dt_zones, "dir", glob=""** [press *enter*]. For example: **batch_fix_dt_zones, "/training/Index_Tiles/" glob="*.pbd"** [press

Table 15. Fix Universal Transverse Mercator or Quarter Quadrangle zones.

Feature	Functionality
"dir"	The input directory for the .pbds.
glob=""	Searches for the files to fix [for example, **glob="*rcf*.pbd"**]. The default search pattern is "*.pbd"

enter].

To zone fix QQ data tiles, type in the command line: **help, batch_fix_qq_zones**. To run the function, type in the command line in this specific order: **batch_fix_qq_zones, "dir", glob=""** [press *enter*]. For example: **batch_fix_qq_zones, "/training/Index_Tiles/" glob="*.pbd"** [press *enter*].

Keep/Remove/Elevation Clipper Filter Tools

When working with topographic data, water areas should be removed (fig. 24); if editing submerged topography, the deeper sections in the data should be removed. This can be done by using the *Keep* or *Remove* filter tools. *Remove* will delete all of the data within the selected region. *Keep* will keep all of the data within the selected region.

When working within a bounded area, such as National Park Service (NPS) boundaries, the bounded area should

be loaded behind the data during editing. This will ensure proximity to the boundary without removing too much or too little data.

Remove Tool

To use the *Remove* tool, go to the *Filter tools* drop-down menu in the *Process EAARL Data* window (fig. 26). Confirm that the *Input Variable* and *Data type* are correct. In the *Remove points using* drop-down menu, select *Rubberband Box* or *Points in Polygon*. Click *Go* and click *OK* on the next window that opens. Begin selecting the region to delete. If the tool is used more than once to remove multiple sections of the data, the plotted data will not update to show these deletions until the user clicks *Plot*. The user can undo the last section that was removed with *Points in Polygon*, *Rubberband Box*, and *Single Pixel* methods, but this does not apply when using *PIP-Thresh* removal or *Keep* (fig. 26) methods.

Keep Tool

Using the *Keep* tool is the same as using the *Remove* tool, but the *Keep* tool deletes all of the data outside of the selected polygon (fig. 26). This is helpful in island areas where a small amount of data is kept (fig. 27). Go to the *Filter tools* drop-down menu and select the *Keep* tool (fig. 26). The *Input Variable* and *Output Variable* are labeled the same and match the variable that is being edited. The *Data Type* should also be the same as the *Mode* in the *Process EAARL Data* window. In the *Keep points using* drop-down menu, select *Rubberband Box* or *Points in Polygon*. Click *OK* on the next window that opens. Begin selecting the region to keep. If the tool is used more than once to remove multiple sections of the data, the plotted data will not update to show these deletions until the user clicks *Plot*. It is better to use the *Remove* tool in the case that a mistake is made.

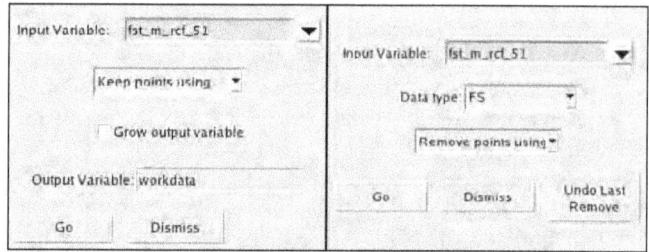

Figure 26. Keep (left) and remove (right) filter windows utilized during manual editing.

PIP-Thresh Removal Tool

The *PIP-Thresh* tool is best utilized in removing outliers displayed in certain sections of the histogram. Go to the *Remove* tool and select *PIP-Thresh* in the *Remove points using* drop-down menu. The *Max. Threshold* is where the maximum

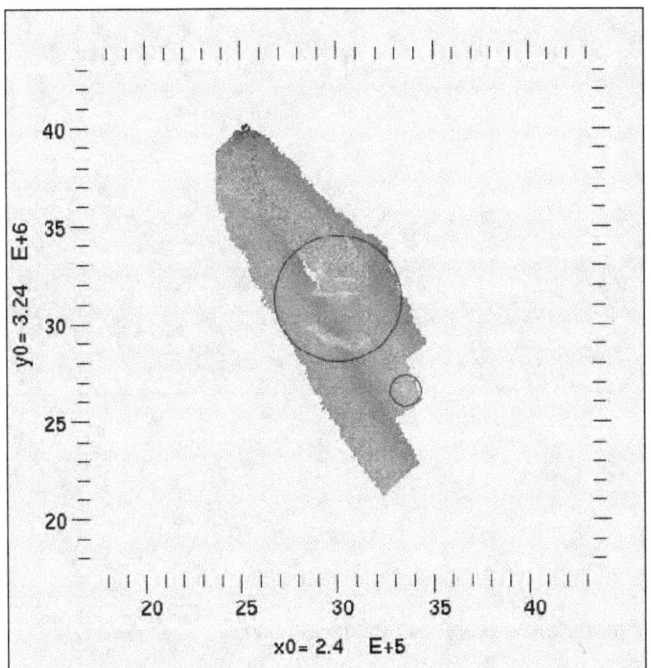

Figure 27. Figure illustrating the use of the keep tool to retain data within the circled areas. Data outside of these areas will be removed.

elevations, *Cmax*, is selected, and the *Min. Threshold* is where the minimum elevation, *Cmin*, is selected. The *PIP-Thresh* tool will remove only the selected points from the current,

Figure 28. A point-cloud elevation histogram shows a well-defined peak near 0 m. Possible outliers located to the left and right of the peak are circled in red.

visible color bar values; for example, if the data are displayed between *Cmin:* -5.00 m and *Cmax:* 0.50 m, then only the data between these values will be removed by the *PIP-Thresh* removal method. The user cannot do this with the *Keep* or other *Remove* tools, which will remove all data within the selected area, whether displayed on the graph or not.

Possible outliers are represented by the flatter sections on either side of the histogram peak (fig. 28). Select the *Histogram Elevations* button and start zooming in to zero on the histogram y-axis until the values range from 10 to -10 measurements. This will exaggerate the elevations at which outliers may occur in the data. Try to ascertain whether the outliers are valid or represent true land features. This can be determined by plotting these areas on the graph and looking at imagery. Sources of imagery to consider include the RGB and CIR imagery that accompanies the EAARL data, Google Earth imagery, or other orthophotography.

Select the "flatter" areas on one side of the histogram peak as the *Cmin* and *Cmax* values. Click *Plot* to display the data points on the graph. If the points appear to be an outlier, click *Go* on the *PIP-Thresh* tool bar. Then select the data to be omitted via a polygon. Ensure that the *Input Variable* is the variable that is being edited. Click the *Histogram Elevations* button again and the specified section of data will be deleted from the rest of the points. Repeat the steps in this section until all of the outliers have been removed from the histogram.

Elevation Clipper Tool

The *Elevation Clipper* is another way to remove outliers on either side of the histogram. Instead of selecting specific points to be removed from the data as with *PIP-Thresh*, this function will "clip" the data on either side of the histogram.

Select the *Histogram Elevations* button and start zooming in to zero on the histogram y-axis until the values range from 10 to -10 measurements. Select *Cmin* and *Cmax* to be displayed on the graph. Click *Plot* to view the data. If the data are outside of the selected histogram limits, they are to be deleted. Click the *Elevation Clipper* button (fig. 29). When the window opens, ensure that the *Input Variable* and the *Output*

Figure 29. The elevation clipper window.

Variable are the same and match the variable that is being edited. Also review the *Minimum Elevation* and *Maximum Elevation* to see that they are the same as the *Cmin* and *Cmax* values on the *Process EAARL Data* window (click *Clip Data*). Click the *Histogram Elevations* button again. Confirm that the data outside of the selected histogram were removed.

Saving Manual Edits

To save edits, select *Write Binary Data File* from the *File* menu on the *Process EAARL Data* window. Select the *Output Path* to be the same as the input path. Add _**mf** to the end of the file name that was edited, then click *Save*. This will save the edited file within the specified directory.

Replace/Datum-Convert Filter Tools

The *Replace* function is used to replace data that were not intended for removal during the filtering process. This often occurs in bare earth data in areas where building density is high and valid, elevated topographic features exist. The filter that was used to filter the last return data to produce a bare earth surface removes most of the buildings. However, valid topographic features surrounding the buildings can be inadvertently removed also.

To replace valid data to the filtered data, load the filtered data. Go to the *Options* menu in the *Process EAARL Data* window and select *Constant Colorbar for Variables*. This will ensure that other loaded variables will have the same color bar values as the data that are being edited. Load in the merge-data file that was created before the filter was applied to the data. This merged file was created from the *write_merge* parameter used during the batch filter process. Go to the *File* menu in the *Process EAARL Data* window, select *Read Binary Data file*, and select the **merged.pbd* file. The file will load into the *Variable* menu as *merged_v*.

If the data being edited have been converted to NAVD88 elevations, then the merged variable must also be converted to NAVD88. Go to the *PostProcessing* menu or the *Filter tools* menu and select *Datum-Convert*. The *Input Variable* should be *merged_v*; if it is not, select it from the drop-down menu and click *Go*. The command terminal may ask for a UTM zone number; enter the zone number at this time. Watch for the return on the command terminal to indicate the datum conversion has finished. Select *n88_merged_v* from the *Variable* list. Unselect the *Auto Fma* button and click *Plot* to have the unfiltered data plotted over the filtered data.

Click the *Filter tools* drop-down menu and select the *Replace* function (fig. 30). The *Original Data Variable* will be the datum converted merged data [*n88_merged_v*] and the *Input Variable* will be the filtered data that needs to be replaced [*bet_m_ircf_m_9*]. Click on the *Same as input variable* button to have the *Output Variable* be the same as the input. The *Output Variable* can be named something else such as *finaldata*. If it is named *finaldata*, this becomes the variable name for the data. In the *Select points to replace using* drop-

Figure 30. The replace function window.

down menu, select *Points in Polygon*, *Rubberband Box*, or *Window Limits*. If prompted, click *OK* on the next window that opens. Select the area of points to be replaced; no selection is required with *Window Limits* function. Click *Filter selected points* and the RCF window appears. Use either the RCF or IRCF filter to edit the area manually. See the Filtering section of this manual for further instructions on using the filter. The filter will use the *Input Variable workdata* and the *Output Variable rcf_workdata*. Click *Go*. The variable *rcf_workdata* will load into the variable list. It is recommended to plot *rcf_workdata* on a graph to determine whether the replacement is an improvement.

If the results are satisfactory, click *Replace*. Click *Yes* in the next window to add the extracted data to the filtered variable. If the results are not satisfactory, click *Do Not Replace* and click *Yes*. Repeat the above steps until all of the removed areas have been replaced.

See the Saving Manual Edits section of this manual to save the edited file.

Quality Control

Accuracy of the produced data depends on the configuration of the lidar system, GPS satellite arrangement, and the type of surface being mapped. Research into the accuracy of the EAARL system has shown that elevation root mean square errors (RMSE) range from 10 to 14 cm for submerged topography to 16 to 20 cm for sub-canopy topography (Nayegandhi and others, 2009). To ensure optimum data accuracy, quality control (QC) procedures have been established. These procedures examine the removal of erroneous points, data anomalies, or any potential horizontal or vertical bias. Anomalies may result from the misalignment of an axis from roll, pitch, or yaw, system timing offsets, atmospheric conditions, GPS bias, or spectral conditions of terrain.

Steps used to the ensure accuracy of the delivered product include: (1) examination of the survey area for errors along the edge of the swath (fig. 31); (2) verification of GPS flight trajectories (fig. 32); (3) use of ground-control data collected along flat/uniformly sloping terrain, not in areas where vegetation is too dense for lidar penetration; (4) use of RMSE calculations between multiple surveys of the same area to estimate both horizontal and vertical accuracy (vertical accuracy of any DEM is defined as 1.96 times RMSE linearly interpolated elevations in the DEM).

First Return Quality Control Specifics

Remove the flat extension on either side of the histogram, if not performed during the manual editing. If reviewing a coastal area, the coastline should be seamless and smooth. Also remove any erroneous data collected during the turn of the aircraft, data that may have been left during the manual editing process. Look at the elevation values to see that the datum conversion worked properly. The vegetation and infrastructure should be included in the first return data; review the data to confirm these are included. If multiple collection days exist, complete the *mtransect* function on a few data tiles. This function will verify the relation between survey days. If there is a difference, it is most likely a GPS

error that exists between the collection days. Review the Determining the Roll Bias section of the manual for directions on the *mtransect* function. After the preceding steps have been completed, add _qc to the end of the filename [*t_e_240000_ n3338000_16_n88_v__b500_w600_n3_merged_fs_rcf_mf_ qc.pbd*].

Bare Earth Quality Control Specifics

Remove the flat extension on either side of the histogram, if not performed during the manual editing. If reviewing a coastal area, the coastline should be seamless and smooth. Remove any erroneous data collected during the turn of the aircraft, data that may have been left during the manual editing process. Review the elevation values to ensure that the datum conversion worked properly. All infrastructure and vegetation should be removed from bare earth data. The filter should remove most of these data, but there could be areas that still need removal after the filter or manual editing. If multiple collection days exist, complete the *mtransect* function on a few data tiles. Review the Determining the Roll Bias section of the manual for directions on the *mtransect* function. If ground-control data exist, find a method of analysis to test data integrity between ground-control data and lidar collection. Compare survey years from the same area. Often data collection occurs over multiple years in the same area to evaluate change. Take an area that is known to be stable over time, such as a parking lot or airport tarmac, then

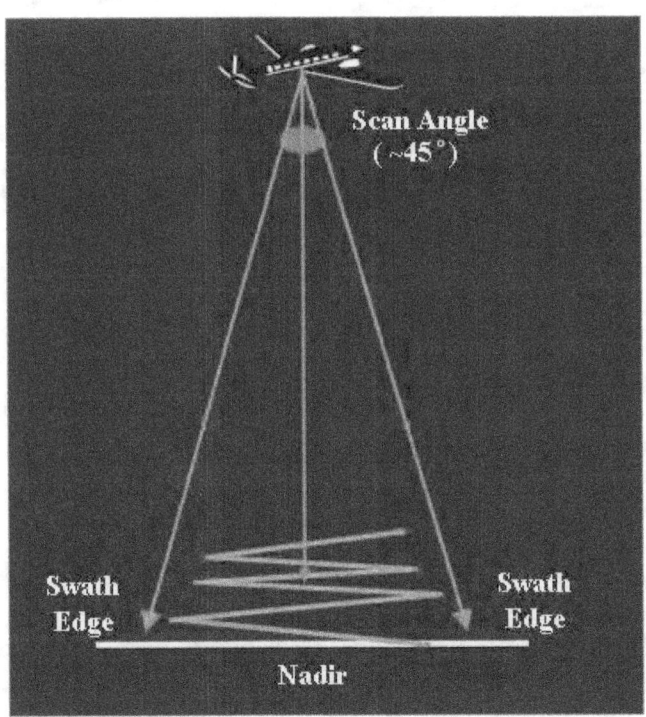

Figure 31. A considerable amount of data can be created along the edge of the swath (Nayegandhi and others, 2006).

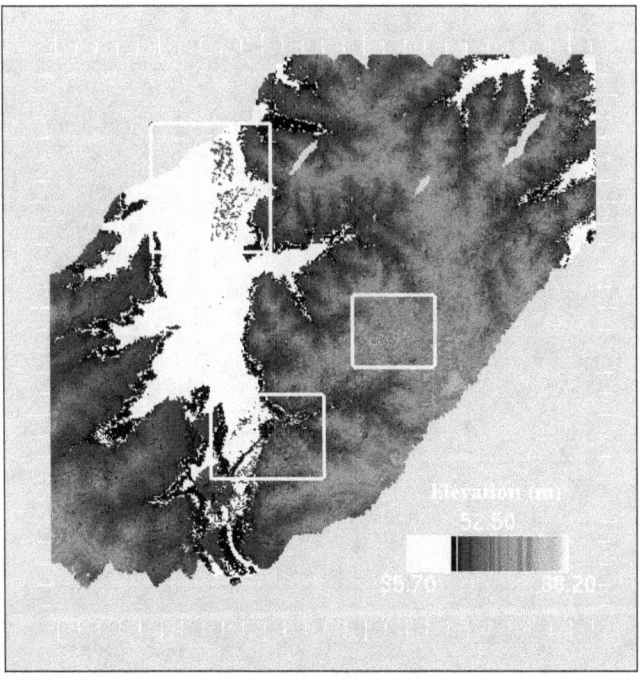

Figure 32. An error in the data can be seen within each square of this bare earth 2-km by 2-km tile. The GPS offset occurred between the 2 days of data collection.

compare these areas against one another. After the preceding steps have been completed, add _qc to the end of the filename [t_e_240000_n3338000_16_n88_v__b500_w60_n3_merged_rcf_mf_qc.pbd].

Product Creation

The final step is to convert the data to point cloud data (ASCII .xyz or ASPRS .las) or grid the data into DEM products. The DEM is usually created by using Delaunay Triangulation, followed by interpolation to create a triangular irregular network (TIN). The output data type is usually a geotiff (32-bit floating-point format) that includes georeferencing information.

Table 16. ASCII XYZ conversion parameters.

Feature	Functionality
"dirname"	Sets the directory name where the input files reside [for example, **"/training/katrina/Index_Tiles/"**].
outdir=""	Set to the output directory name to write files to this location. The default will be the same path as the input directory. Set up a new directory for the ASCII .xyz files [for example, **outdir="/training/katrina/be_xyz/"**].
mode	Set to 1 for the first return, 2 for bathymetry, and 3 for bare earth. This will also append fs, ba, or be into the output file name.
zone	Set to UTM zone number.
ss=""	Searches for data used in the find command. This will override other search options, such as rcfmode, datum, readpbd, and readedf [for example, **ss="*rcf*mf*.pbd"**].
rcfmode	Set to 1 to convert RCF'd files, set to 2 to convert IRCF'd files, and set to 3 to convert IRCF_mf files. This option is considered an alternative to the search string.
buffer	Sets buffer to size in meters. Data outside the tile's limits plus the buffer's size will be excluded. A negative value indicates that all data should be used.
atm	Set to 1 if converting ATM data.
qq	Set to 1 to convert the quarter quadrangle tiles into the ASCII format.
update	Set to 1 to convert only those files that have not been converted to the ASCII .xyz format. This will not affect already converted files.

Conversion to ASCII XYZ Format

To begin the conversion to ASCII .xyz, open the following windows: ytk, eaarl, and Process EAARL Data. (See the Opening ALPS Processing Windows section for instruction.) Set the curzone/utmzone [for example, **curzone=16** or **utmzone=16**]. Type in the command line: **help, batch_write_xyz**. Alternatively, go to batch_write_xyz within the CmdLine menu in the Process EAARL Data window. This will open a help document explaining which parameters should be included in the conversion to ASCII .xyz (table 16).

Once the appropriate parameters have been determined, type the following command: **batch_write_xyz, "dirname", outdir="", mode=, zone=, ss="", buffer=** [press enter]. For example: **batch_write_xyz, "/training/Index_Tiles/", outdir= "/training/fs_xyz/", mode=1, zone=16, ss="*fs*_qc.pbd", buffer=10** [press enter].

Other options can be used when converting .pbd data to ASCII .xyz; review the help document for those options. Upon function completion, a return will appear in the command prompt.

Conversion to ASPRS LAS Format

In order to begin the ASPRS .las conversion, open the following windows: ytk, eaarl, and Process EAARL Data. (See the Opening ALPS Processing Windows section for instruction. Set the curzone/utmzone [for example, **curzone=16** or **utmzone=16**]. Type in the command line **help, batch_pbd2las**. Alternatively, go to batch_pbd2las within the CmdLine menu in the Process EAARL Data window. This will

Table 17. ASPRS LAS conversion parameters.

Feature	Functionality
"con_dir"	The directory name where the input files reside [for example, **"/training/katrina/Index_Tiles/"**].
searchstr=""	Searches for data used in the find command [for example, **searchstr="*rcf*mf*.pbd"**]. This will override other search options such as nad83, wgs84N, and wgs84S.
zone_nbr	Sets the UTM zone number
typ	Set to 1 if converting first return, 2 for bare earth, and 3 for submerged topography.
buffer	Specifies buffer in meters used to apply to tile boundary. If set to -1 (default), all data will be used.
qq	Set to 1 to convert quarter quadrangle tiles into ASPRS .las format.
update	Set to 1 to process only those files that have not been converted to a ASPRS .las format. This will not affect already converted files.

open a help document explaining which parameters should be included in the conversion to ASPRS *.las* (table 17).

Once the appropriate parameters have been determined, type the following command: **batch_pbd2las, "con_dir", searchstr="", zone_nbr=, typ=, buffer=** [press *enter*]. For example: **batch_pbd2las, "/training/Index_Tiles/", searchstr="*fs*_qc.pbd", zone_nbr=16, typ=1, buffer=10** [press *enter*].

Other options can be used when converting to ASPRS *.las*; review the help document for those options. Upon function completion, a return [>] will appear in the command prompt.

A series of scripts has been created for the interactive data language (IDL) to read EAARL data format (*.edf*) files created in ALPS, triangulate them based on area and distance thresholds, and create a grid based on the triangulation.

In order to begin the *.pbd* to *.edf* batch conversion, open the following windows: *ytk*, *eaarl*, and *Process EAARL Data*. (See the Opening ALPS Processing Windows section for instruction.) Begin in ALPS by converting the manually edited *.pbd* into *.edf*. Type in the command line: **#include "batch_typ_convert.i"**, then type **help, batch_pbd2edf** to open the help document listing possible parameters (table 18). Type the following command: **batch_pbd2edf, "dirname", searchstr=""** [press *enter*]. For example: **batch_pbd2edf, "/training/Index_Tiles/", searchstr="*_qc.pbd"** [press *enter*].

Table 18. pbd2edf conversion parameters.

Feature	Functionality
"dirname"	The directory name where the input files reside [for example, **"/training/katrina/Index_Tiles/"**].
searchstr=""	Searches for data in the find command [for example, **searchstr="*rcf*mf*.pbd"**]. This will override other search options, such as rcfmode, onlymf, n88, and w84.

Upon function completion, a return [>] will appear in the command terminal. The *.edf* files are ready for use in IDL (as long as IDL is installed). Open another shell or terminal in Linux. The user must migrate to the following directory to begin processing: **cd /opt/eaarl/lidar-processing/idl** [press *enter*]. Once in the directory, type **idlde**; the user will then see IDL load. Go to the *File* menu and click *Open*. A window will open with scripts; select the following: *batch_grid.pro* and *grid_eaarl_data.pro* [click *OK*]. Go to the *Run* menu and select *Compile All*. The processing window will state *Compiled module: BATCH_GRID, BATCH_MAKE_GE_PLOTS, GRID_EAARL_DATA, PLOT_EAARL_GRIDS, PLOT_ZBUF_EAARL_GRIDS, MAKE_GE_PLOTS, and WRITE_GEOTIFF.* The parameters will display in the top main window (table 19). Type the following command in the *IDL>* command line: **batch_grid, "directory", write_geotiffs=1, utmzone=, mode=,**

Table 19. Interactive Data Language DEM creation parameters.

Feature	Functionality
"filename"	The directory name where the input files reside [for example, **"/training/katrina/Index_Tiles/"**].
cell	Sets the grid cell dimension. The default is 1 m.
mode	Set to 1 for the first surface, 2 for bathymetry, and 3 for bare earth.
searchstr=""	Searches for data used in the find command [for example, **searchstr="*rcf*mf*.edf"**].
write_geotiffs	Set to 1 to write out geotiffs.
utmzone	Sets UTM zone number.
area_threshold	This is the maximum allowable area of a triangulated facet. The default for this value is 200 square meters.
dist_threshold	This is the maximum allowable distance between two vertices of the triangulated facet. The default for this value is 50 meters. Increase this value to reduce "holes" in the data.

searchstr="" [press *enter*]. For example: **batch_grid, "/training/Index_Tiles/", write_geotiffs=1, utmzone=16, mode=1, searchstr="*.edf"** [press *enter*].

Other options can be used when gridding; review the script for those options. The processing window will inform the user of gridding completion.

GlobalMapper DEM Creation

ALPS 2-km Data Tile DEM Creation

A script has been created for the geographic information system (GIS) software GlobalMapper™ to read the three-dimensional point data (ASCII *.xyz*), triangulate it, and create a grid based on the triangulation. The script eliminates points from the grid by comparing the distance from each point to a real data point. The threshold value establishes the distance to a real data point. This value controls the gaps within and along the edges of the dataset. The edges are problematic areas. Large triangles can be created to cover a large spatial area in which no real data points exist. The threshold will tell the script how close to trim those areas. If the threshold is made too small, then areas of points become isolated rather than becoming a smooth product. If the threshold is made too large, then a "collar" begins to form around the data.

To be able to use the *gm_xyz2dem* script, Active TCL (Version 8.4.17.0) and GlobalMapper must be installed. Double click on the *gm_xyz2dem* script and a window will

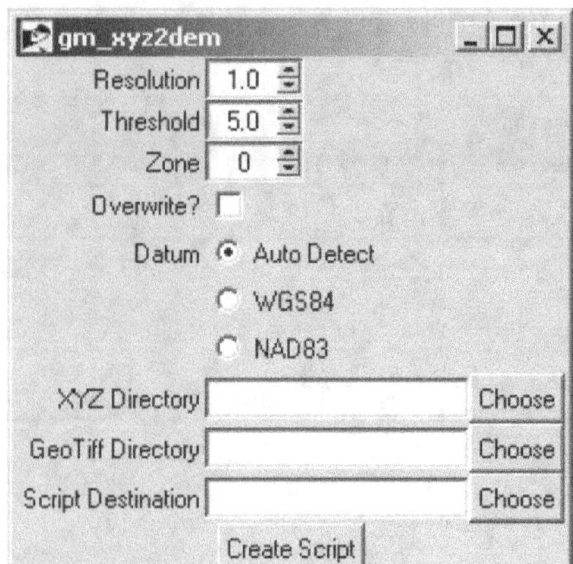

Figure 33. Window that shows DEM script created for GlobalMapper.

Table 20. Quarter Quadrangle geotiff preparation parameters.

Feature	Functionality
"tif_dir"	Designates the location of the 2-km geotiff directory [for example, **"/training/katrina/be_ geotiff/"**].
"pbd_dir"	Designates the location of the QQ .pbd directory [for example, **"/training/katrina/be_QQ_ tiles/"**].
mode	Set as 1 for the first surface, 2 for bathymetry, and 3 for bare earth.
outfile	Generates the output file [for example, **"~/ katrina05be.tcl"**]. This file is used in the geotiff creation.
tif_glob=""	Searches for specific .tif files from data directory. Default is *.tif.
pbd_glob=""	Searches for specific .pbd files from data quarter quadrangle directory. Default is *.pbd.

open (fig. 33). Keep the following values the same: *Resolution* at 1, *Threshold* at 5; the zone and datum will automatically be detected from the file names. This script will only work for data tiles in the 2-km by 2-km data tile format. See the Quarter Quadrangle Data Tile DEM Creation section of this manual to convert QQ data into DEMs. Click the *Choose* button to select an input directory of ASCII *.xyz* data for the *XYZ Directory* and then to select an output directory for the *GeoTiff Directory*. For the *Script Destination*, name the script and click on the *Choose* button to select the location of the script. Remember the script location because it will be used again. Add **.gms** to the end of the script name [for example, *runme.gms*]. Once the script is saved, click the *Create Script* button. A window will appear with *Your script has been created*. Open GlobalMapper and go to the *File* menu and click *Run Script*. Navigate to the directory where the saved *.gms* script is located and select it. The script processing window opens. Click *Run Script* button. This process will take approximately 15 minutes to run. When it has finished, click *close*.

Open the newly created DEM files in GlobalMapper by clicking *Open your own data files* or go to the *File* menu and click *Open Data File(s)*. Navigate to the designated output directory and the files are displayed.

Quarter Quadrangle Data Tile DEM Creation

To create DEMs from QQ-formatted data, convert the EAARL or ATM data into 2-km data tiles. (See the section on Quarter Quadrangle to ALPS 2-km Conversion.) To create geotiffs, complete the steps in Interactive Data Language DEM Creation. Copy the geotiffs into a separate directory and then onto a local machine. Review all geotiffs and delete any that are empty. Solid red or black squares represent empty

geotiffs. Sync changes back to the original location. Manually delete the files at the original location or use **rsync --delete**. Ensure that there are quarter quadrangle *.pbd* files. Type **help, qqtiff_gms_prep** to open the help document (table 20). Type the following command: **qqtiff_gms_prep, "tif_dir", "pbd_dir", mode, "outfile"** [press *enter*]. For example: **qqtiff_gms_prep, "/training//2k_fs_geotiffs/",, "/training/fs_QQ", 1, "/training/ katrina.tcl"** [press *enter*].

Transfer the output file to a local machine. Copy the *gm_tiff2ktoqq.tcl* script from the */opt/eaarl/lidar-processing/ linux-xp* directory to a local machine. To be able to use the *gm_tiff2ktoqq.tcl* script, Active TCL (Version 8.4.17.0) and GlobalMapper must be installed. Double click on the *gm_tiff2ktoqq.tcl* script and a window will open (fig. 34). Click *Choose* in the *2k Tiff Source Path*, navigate to the geotiff source directory. Click *OK*. Click *Choose* in the *QQ Tiff Destination Path*, navigate to a created QQ directory. Click *OK*. The *Output Naming Scheme* specifies a prefix and a suffix to use for the output geotiff filenames. The light gray *12345a6b* is a placeholder to show where the quarter quadrangle names

Figure 34. Window that shows GlobalMapper geotiff conversion script.

will go. Fields may be left blank. Click *Choose* in the *Data File*, navigate to the created *qqtiff_gms_prep* script. Click *OK*. Click *Choose* in the *Script Destination*, navigate to the output directory for the GlobalMapper script, and give the script a filename. Click *OK*. Click *Generate Global Mapper Script*. A window will open with *Your script has been created*. The dialog will *not* close, click the *X* in the top right corner of the dialog to exit.

Open GlobalMapper and go to the *File* menu and click *Run Script*. Navigate to the directory where the saved *.gms* script is located and select it. The script processing window opens. Click *Run Script* button. This process will take approximately 15 minutes to run. When it has finished, click *close*. Open the newly created DEM files in GlobalMapper by clicking *Open your own data files* or go to the *File* menu and click *Open Data File(s)*. Navigate to the designated output directory and the files are displayed.

References Cited

Brock, J.C., Wright, C.W., Clayton, T.D., Nayegandhi, Amar, 2004, LIDAR optical rugosity of coral reefs in Biscayne National Park, Florida: Coral Reefs, v. 23, p. 48-59.

Fischler, M.A., and Bolles, R.C., 1981, Random sample consensus: A paradigm for model fitting with applications to image analysis and automated cartography: Communications of the Association for Computing Machinery, v. 24, p. 381-395.

Harris, M., Brock, J.C., Nayegandhi, Amar, and Duffy, M., 2005, Extracting shorelines from NASA airborne topographic lidar-derived digital elevation models: U.S. Geological Survey Open-File Report 2005-1427, 32 p.

Nayegandhi, Amar, Brock, J.C., and Wright C.W., 2009, Small-footprint, waveform-resolving lidar estimation of submerged and sub-canopy topography in coastal environments: International Journal of Remote Sensing, v. 30, no. 4, p. 861-878.

Nayegandhi, Amar, Brock, J.C., Wright C.W., Clayton, T.D., and Mosher, L.A., 2004, Processing and Filtering 'Bare Earth' Topographic Data Acquired by NASA's Experimental Advanced Airborne Research Lidar (EAARL), *in* Proceedings of the American Society for Photogrammetry and Remote Sensing (ASPRS) Annual Conference, Denver, CO, 23-28 May 2004, one CD-ROM.

Nayegandhi, Amar, Brock, J.C., Wright, C.W., and O'Connell, M.J., 2006, Evaluating a small footprint, waveform-resolving lidar over coastal vegetation communities: Photogrammetric Engineering & Remote Sensing, v. 72, no. 12, p. 1407-1417.

Sallenger, A.H., and Brock, J.C., 2001, Coastal change hazards during extreme storms investigated with airborne topographic lidar: U.S. Geological Survey Open-File Report 01-98, 2 p.

Shrestha, R., Carter, W., Slatton, C., and Dietrich, W., 2007, "Research-quality" airborne laser swath mapping: The defining factors: LEN – LiDAR Remote Sensing Education Network, Geosensing Engineering and Mapping (GEM) Civil and Coastal Engineering Department University of Florida, accessed on: 1 January 2008. URL: http://www.aspl.ece.ufl.edu/reports/NCALM_WhitePaper_v1.1.pdf.

Wagner, W., Ullrich, A., Melzer T., Briese, C., and Kraus, K., 2004, From single-pulse to full-waveform airborne laser scanners: Potential and practical challenges: International Archives of Photogrammetry and Remote Sensing, v. 35, Part B3, p. 201-206.

Wagner, W., Roncat, A., Melzer, T., and Ullrich, A., 2007, Waveform analysis techniques in airborne laser scanning: International Archives of Photogrammetry and Remote Sensing, v. 36, Part 3, p. 413-418.

Wright, C.W., and Brock, J.C., 2002, EAARL: A lidar for mapping shallow coral reefs and other coastal environments, *in* Proceedings of the Seventh International Conference on Remote Sensing for Marine and Coastal Environments, Miami, FL, 20-22 May 2002, Veridian International Conferences, one CD-ROM.

Appendix A. ALPS Installation

This section documents the steps needed to install ALPS and its required software on a computer running Linux. These instructions require root or superuser access to the machine.

1. Set up directories.
   a. Create the following directories for the ALPS system:
      sudo mkdir -p /opt/eaarl
      sudo chown `id –un `.`id -gn` /opt/eaarl
      mkdir -p /opt/eaarl/packages/src
      mkdir /opt/eaarl/bin
   b. Create the following directory and download into the directory all of the files required for the rest of the document.
      mkdir /opt/eaarl/tarfiles

2. ActiveTcl
   a. Download *ActiveTcl 8.4.17.0* from the website. Select the *-x86_64.tar.gz* file for a 64-bit system. Otherwise, select the *-ix86.tar.gz* file (most installers will use this). http://downloads.activestate.com/ActiveTcl/Linux/8.4.17/
   b. Untar the tarball as a directory in /opt/eaarl/packages/src/.
      cd /opt/eaarl/packages/src
      tar zxvf /opt/eaarl/tarfiles/ActiveTcl8.4.17-linux-ix86.tar.gz
   c. Run the install script for ActiveTcl. When prompted for an installation location, choose /opt/eaarl/packages/ActiveTcl8.4.17.
      cd ActiveTcl8.4.17-linux-ix86
      ./install.sh
   d. Add these links to ActiveTcl in the /opt/eaarl/bin/ directory:
      cd /opt/eaarl/bin
      ln -sf /opt/eaarl/packages/ActiveTcl8.4.17/bin/page
      ln -sf /opt/eaarl/packages/ActiveTcl8.4.17/bin/tclsh
      ln -sf /opt/eaarl/packages/ActiveTcl8.4.17/bin/tclsh8.4
      ln -sf /opt/eaarl/packages/ActiveTcl8.4.17/bin/teacup
      ln -sf /opt/eaarl/packages/ActiveTcl8.4.17/bin/tkcon
      ln -sf /opt/eaarl/packages/ActiveTcl8.4.17/bin/wish
      ln -sf /opt/eaarl/packages/ActiveTcl8.4.17/bin/wish8.4

3. rlwrap
   a. Download rlwrap from the lidar.net server.lidar.net:/mnt/alps/eaarl/tarfiles/rlwrap-0.21.tar.gz
   b. Untar the tarball as a directory in /opt/eaarl/packages/src.
      cd /opt/eaarl/packages/src
      tar zxvf /opt/eaarl/tarfiles/rlwrap-0.21.tar.gz
   c. Compile and install.
      cd rlwrap-0.21
      ./configure --prefix=/opt/eaarl
      make
      make install

4. Yorick
   a. Download *Yorick 2.1.04* from lidar.net.
      lidar.net:/mnt/alps/eaarl/tarfiles/yorick-2.1.04.tgz
   b. Untar the tarball as a directory in */opt/eaarl/packages/src/*.
      cd /opt/eaarl/packages/src
      tar zxvf /opt/eaarl/tarfiles/yorick-2.1.04.tgz
   c. Build yorick.
      cd yorick-2.1.04
      make relocatable
   d. Install yorick.
      cd /opt/eaarl/packages
      tar zxvf /opt/eaarl/packages/src/yorick-2.1.04/yorick-2.1-04.tgz
   e. Add links to yorick in */opt/eaarl/bin*.
      cd /opt/eaarl/bin
      ln -sf /usr/local/yorick-2.1-04/bin/yorick
      ln -sf /usr/local/yorick-2.1-04/bin/gist

5. Yorick-Z
   a. Download *Yorick-Z 1.2* from lidar.net.
      lidar.net:/mnt/alps/eaarl/tarfiles/yorick-z-1.2.tgz
   b. Untar the tarball as a directory in */opt/eaarl/packages/src/*.
      cd /opt/eaarl/packages/src
      tar zxvf /opt/eaarl/tarfiles/yorick-z-1.2.tgz
   c. Compile and install.
      cd yorick-z-1.2
      ./configure
      make
      make check
      make install

6. Yeti
   a. Download *Yeti 6.2.1* from lidar net.
      lidar.net:/mnt/alps/eaarl/tarfiles/yeti-6.2.1.tar.gz
   b. Untar the tarball as a directory in */opt/eaarl/packages/src.*
      cd /opt/eaarl/packages/src
      tar zxvf /opt/eaarl/tarfiles/yeti-6.2.1.tar.gz
   c. Compile and install.
      cd yeti-6.2.1
      yorick -batch ./config i
      make
      make install

7. YTK
    a. Download *YTK 1.0a* from lidar.net.
       lidar.net:/mnt/alps/eaarl/tarfiles/ytk-1.0a.tgz
    b. Untar the tarball as a directory in */opt/eaarl/
       packages/src.*
       cd /opt/eaarl/packages/src
       tar zxvf /opt/eaarl/tarfiles/ytk-1.0a.tgz
    c. Copy the required files to their appropriate places.
       cd ytk-1.0a
       **mkdir /opt/eaarl/packages/yorick-2.1.04/
       contrib**
       **cp ytk.i /opt/eaarl/packages/yorick-2.1.04/
       contrib/**
       **cp ytk.gif /opt/eaarl/packages/yorick-2.1.04/
       contrib/**

8. ALPS
    a. Obtain *ALPS*, either through Concurrent Version
       Systems (CVS) or as a tarball, and install as */opt/
       eaarl/lidar-processing.* For the tarball:
       cd /opt/eaarl
       tar zxvf /opt/eaarl/tarfiles/alps.tar.gz
    b. Build and install the ALPS yorick plugins.
       cd /opt/eaarl/lidar-processing/yorick-extend/rcf
       yorick -batch make i
       make
       make install
       make clean

9. GEOID Files
    a. Obtain the *GEOID* files from lidar.net.
       *lidar.net:/mnt/alps/eaarl/tarfiles/geoid03_
       pbdfiles.tgz*
    b. Untar the tarball as a directory in */opt/eaarl/lidar-
       processing.*
       cd /opt/eaarl/lidar-processing
       tar zxvf /opt/eaarl/tarfiles/geoid03_pbdfiles.tgz

Appendix B. Virtual Network Computing

Virtual Network Computing (VNC) is a remote desktop application that allows a connection to a remote computer, as if it were accessed from a keyboard. It consists of two main components: the viewer and the server. The computer to which the user is connected is called the *server*, and the computer from which the user is connected is the *viewer*. The *viewer* is a small application (150 kilobytes for Win32 version) that allows a remote PC to connect to the server, as well as the ability to view or control the server desktop. The *server* requires installation of the VNC Service plus the installation of VNC hooks via a registry file. The low-bandwidth requirements permit VNC to run on a wide range of hardware.

To begin a Virtual Network Computing session:

1.   Open a secure shell (SSH)connection.

2.   Create a profile under *Profiles* menu on the SSH prompt (or click on a previously created profile). Name the profile for the computer that is to be connected.

3.   Edit the profile.

   a) Click on the *Profiles* menu.

   b) Click *Edit Profile….*

   c) Enter the *Host name* and *User name*.

       [for example, *Host name:* **computername.er.usgs. gov** and *User name:* **jboniste**].

   d) Message from the server will appear [click *OK*].

4.   Enter the password for computer [click *OK*].

5.   Type in the command line **vncserver**.

6.   The command line will state, "New computername. er.usgs.gov:# (username) desktop is computername. er.usgs.gov:#: [for example, *New asterix.er.usgs. gov:1 (jboniste) desktop is asterix.er.usgs.gov:1*].

7.   Open a VNC connection.

8.   Enter the specified starting application as **computername: #** [for example, **asterix:1**].

9.   Click *connect*.

10.   Enter password. This VNC connection remains unless the connection is somehow killed.

11.   When finished, shut down the server. To close a VNC server, type in the SSH prompt:

vncserver -kill :# [for example, **vncserver -kill :1**]. SSH will state "Killing Xvnc process ID ####" [for example, *Killing Xvnc process ID 5065*].

12.   If the VNC viewing screen is too large or small, it can be modified by changing the aliases located in the .cshrc file of the user's home directory. The syntax for creating an alias on the command line is:

alias vs vncserver –alwaysshared –depth 16 –geom- etry

The change will only affect new terminal sessions when vs is typed in the SSH command line.

To reflect in a terminal session that is al- ready open, type this command:
source ~/.cshrc

Appendix C. Typical EAARL Raw Directory Setup

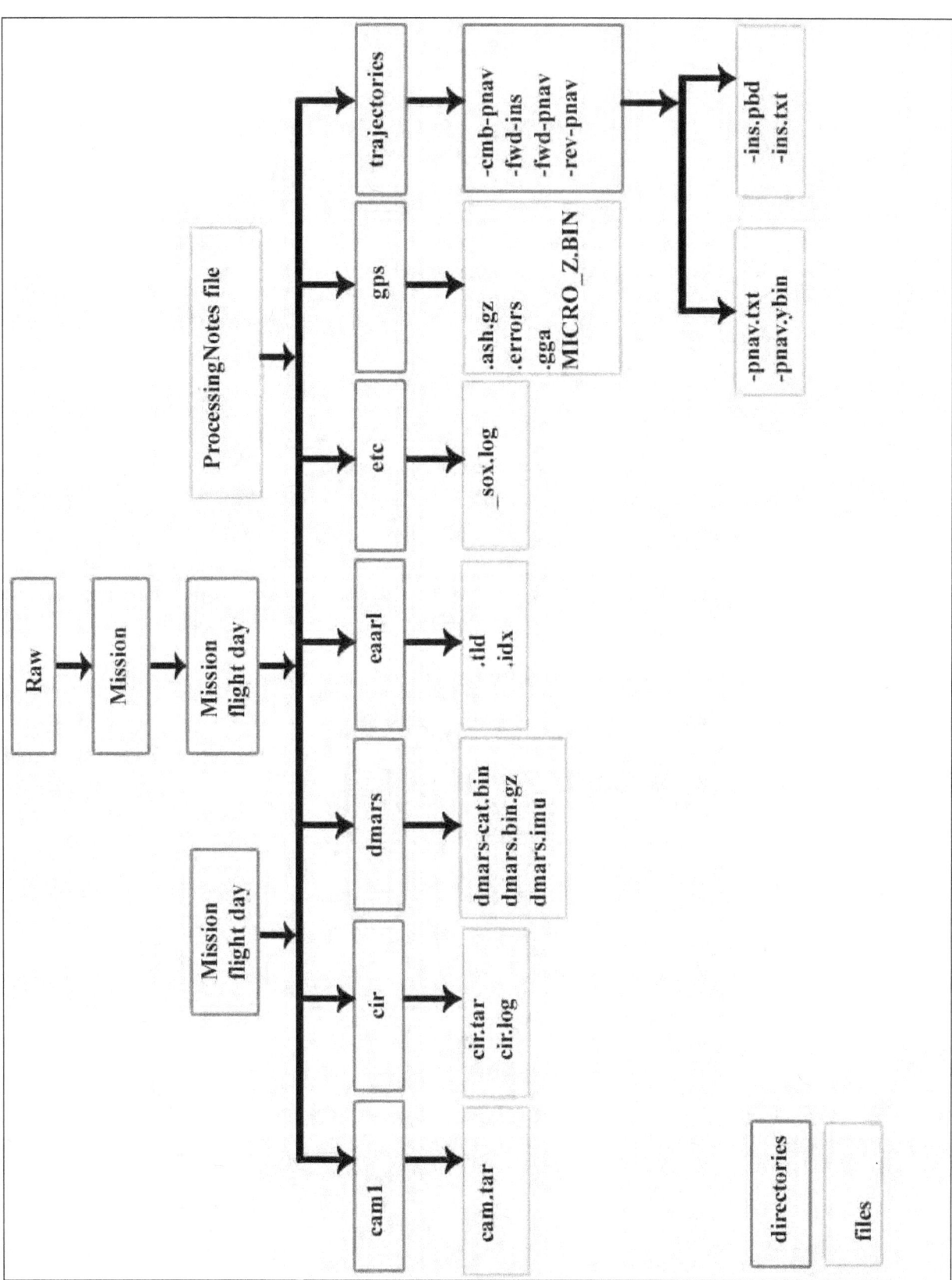

Appendix D. Major EAARL Data Processing Steps

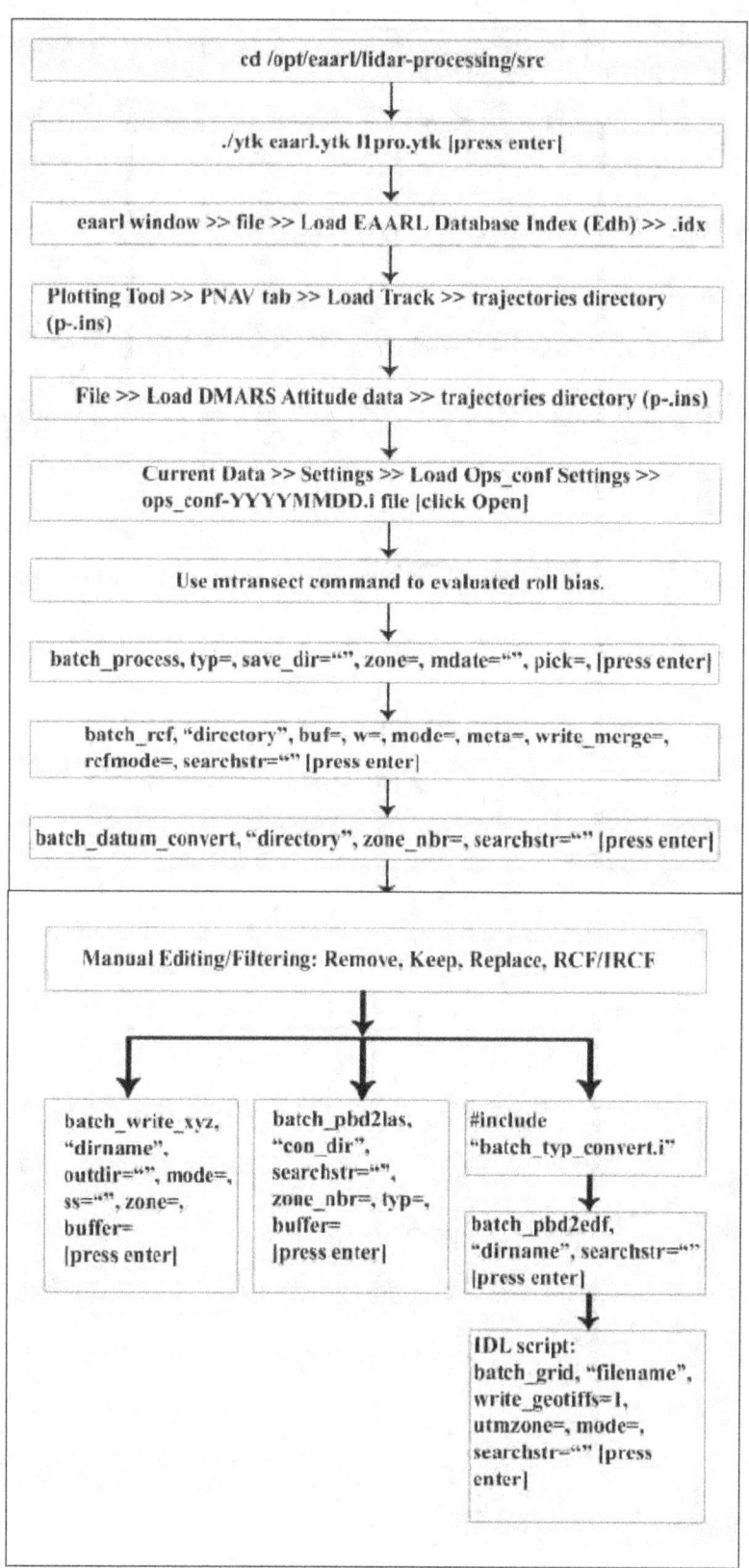

Appendix E: Additional Processing Information

Other processing modes include:

a)   *Direct. Wave Spectra* displays the dominant wave propagation for the submerged topography data area. The resulting windows appear after the processing has been completed (fig. 35).

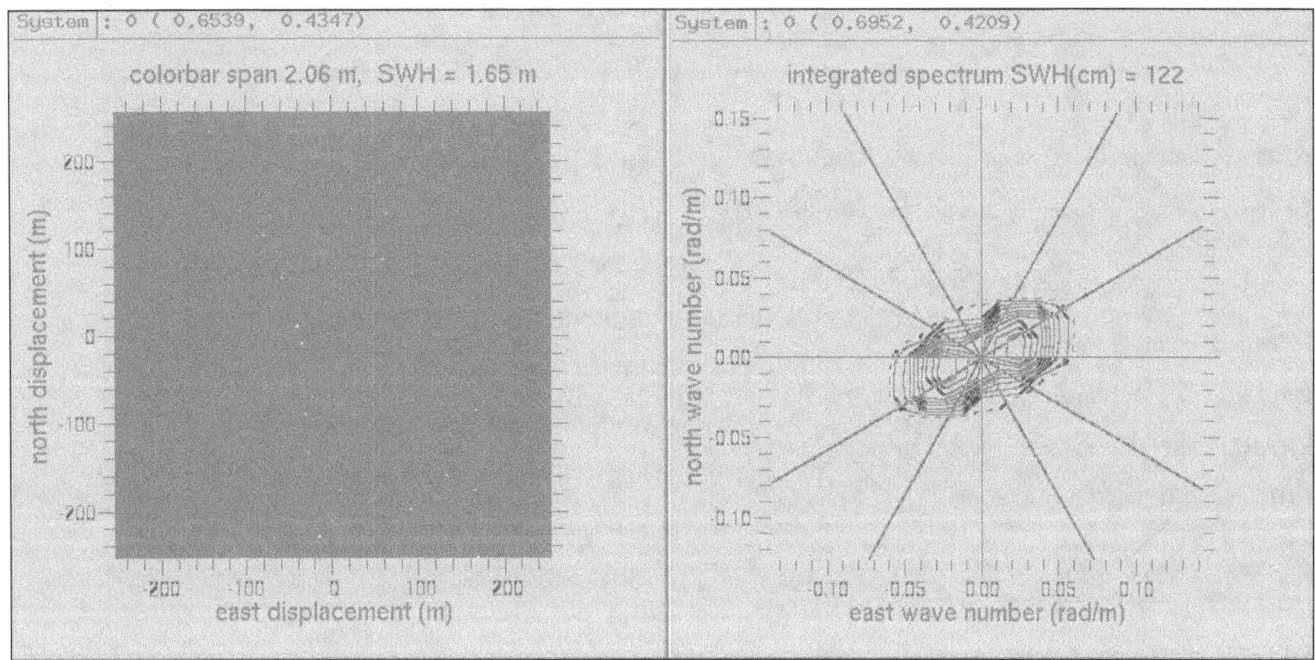

Figure 35. Directional wave spectra display.

b)   *Multi Peak Veg* displays processed discrete-return lidar system data. EAARL is not a discrete system but a waveform-resolving lidar system. This processing mode is not available for evaluating EAARL lidar data.

List of Abbreviations and Acronyms

AGL – Above Ground Level

ALPS – Airborne Lidar Processing System

ASCII – American Standard Code for Information Interchange

ASPRS – American Society for Photogrammetry and Remote Sensing

ATM – Airborne Topographic Mapper

CIN – Image Index

CIR – Color-Infrared

CLICK – Center for Lidar Information Coordination and Knowledge

CVS – Concurrent Versions System

DEM – Digital Elevation Model

DMARS – Digital Miniature Attitude Reference System

EAARL – Experimental Advanced Airborne Research Lidar

EDB – EAARL DataBase index file

EDF – EAARL Data Format

GeoTIFF – Georeferenced Tagged Image File Format

GIS – Geographic Information Systems

GPS – Global Positioning System

HMS – Hours Minutes Seconds

IDL – Interactive Data Language

IMU – Inertial Measurement Unit

IRCF – Iterative Random Consensus Filter

JPEG – Joint Photographic Experts Group (Compressed Photographic Images)

KML – Keyhole Markup Language (Google Code)

KMZ – Keyhole Markup Language Zipped (Compressed KML files)

LAS – Log ASCII Standard

lidar – Light Detection And Ranging

NAD83 – North American Datum of 1983

NASA – National Aeronautic and Space Administration

NAVD88 – North American Vertical Datum of 1988

NGS – National Geodetic Survey

NPS – National Park Service

PBD – Processed EAARL Files in Yorick

PDOP – Position Dilution of Precision

PIP – Points In a Polygon

PMT – Photomultiplier Tube

PNAV – Precision Navigation

PNG – Portable Network Graphics

QA – Quality Assurance

QC – Quality Control

QQ – Quarter Quadrangle

RANSAC – Random Sample Consensus

RCF – Random Consensus Filter

RGB – Red-Green-Blue

RMSE – Root Mean Square Error

SOD – Seconds Of the Day

SOW – Seconds Of the Week

SSH – Secure Shell

TIFF – Tagged Image File Format

TIN – Triangulated Irregular Network

USGS – U.S. Geological Survey

UTM – Universal Transverse Mercator

VNC – Virtual Network Computing

WGS84 – World Geodetic System 1984

WGS84 G1150 – World Geodetic System 1984 Precise Ephemeris Beginning GPS Week 1150

YAG – Yttrium Aluminum Garnet

Bonisteel, et al—Experimental Advanced Airborne Reasearch Lidar (EAARL) Data Processing Manual— Open File Report Series 2009-1078